Dalton Square Medical Ltd

Also available...

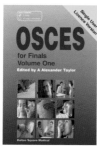   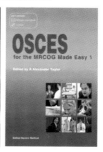

Seven Steps to Success by S.J.Duthie
ISBN 978-0-9555690-4-3
A Guide to the Part 2 MRCOG by S.J.Duthie
ISBN 978-0-9555690-3-6
Hysterectomy An Interactive CD-ROM Teaching Aid
ISBN 978-0-9541732-1-X
OSCES for the MRCOG Made Easy Volume 1 (trainee version)
ISBN 978-0-9541732-2-8
OSCES for Finals Volume 1 (single user version)
ISBN 978-0-9541732-7-9
OSCES for Nurses Volume 1 (single user version)
ISBN 978-0-9555690-0-5
OSCES for the MRCOG Made Easy Volume 2 (Home Edition)
ISBN 978-0-9555690-1-2

You can order titles, from your local bookshop or directly from Dalton Square Medical at
www.Daltonsquaremedical.co.uk

A Guide to entry into Specialty Training in Obstetrics & Gynaecology

Edited by

A Alexander Taylor

Published by Dalton Square Medical Ltd

First published 2010

ISBN 978-0-9555690-6-7

British Library Cataloguing in Publication Data
A catalogue record for this book is available from the British Library

Library of Congress Cataloguing in Publication Data
A catalogue record for this book is available from the Library of Congress

Note
Medical knowledge is constantly changing. As new information becomes available, changes in treatment, procedures, equipment and the use of drugs become necessary. The editor, contributors and the publishers have, as far as it is possible, taken care to ensure that the information given in this text is accurate and up to date. However, readers are strongly advised to confirm that the information, especially with regard to drug usage, complies with the latest legislation and standards of practice.

Printed in England by Colin Cross Printers 01995 604368

Contents

Contributors

Susan Ward FRCS(Ed) DM FRCOG
Consultant Obstetrician & Gynaecologist
Training Programme Director for East Midlands (north)
Sherwood Forest Hospitals NHS Trust, Nottingham

Alec McEwan BA BM BCh MRCOG
RCOG College Tutor, Consultant Obstetrician & Gynaecologist
Queen's Medical Centre Campus, Nottingham

Jo Mountfield MA MBChB FRCOG
Consultant Obstetrician and Director of Education Southampton University
Head of School for Obstetrics & Gynaecology, Wessex Deanery

A Alexander Taylor MBBS MRCOG MD
Consultant Obstetrician & Gynaecologist
Royal Bournemouth & Christchurch Hospitals, Bournemouth

Aarti Umranikar MRCOG MFFP
Specialist Registrar
Queen Anne's, Southampton

Krupa Madhvani MBBS
Specialist Registrar, Queen Anne's, Southampton

Sasha Paul
The Dramatic Solution, Bournemouth

Rosie Thorpe
The Dramatic Solution, Bournemouth

Molly Jackson
The Dramatic Solution, Bournemouth

Joseph Carole
ANA Actors, London

Matthew Huggins
Deputy Head of Postgraduate Training, The Royal College of Obstetricians &
Gynaecologists

Dedications

This booklet and accompanying videos
are dedicated to Daisy & Sebastian

Acknowledgements

The materials used in sections 1.3, 1.4, 1.5, 1.7 and 1.8 have all been directly taken from the information available on the ObsJobs website, which can be found at https://obsjobs.rcog.org.uk/. These materials are all protected by copyright and are reproduced here with the kind permission of the Royal College of Obstetricians and Gynaecologists. The 'General Information' page on the site (https://obsjobs.rcog. org.uk/info/general_info) contains further information, such as an FAQ document, the number of posts available per deanery and the relevant interview dates, and is updated with relevant information throughout the recruitment process. Please note that the person specifications, application form and other information may change for each recruitment round. The latest information can always be found on the ObsJobs website and this site should always be consulted as the primary information source for recruitment information.

To Elspeth and David Hopkins for their help

proofreading, to Martin for his Design work,

to Toby for his help with video production

and Jane Moody RCOG.

Part 1

Chapter 1
Approaching the application form

by Susan Ward, Training Programme Director for East Midlands

The application form is your ticket to the interview. Like your curriculum vitae, your application form is the "shop window" that sells you to the selectors as someone who has the interest, dedication and capability to be trained to consultant level in seven years time – a tall order! With your answers you are trying to convince the reader that they should invite you to the interview because you are likely to be just what they are looking for.

When the Royal College of General Practitioners was trying to improve their selection process some years ago they started with a "wish list" of the attributes any patient would like to see in their GP (obvious things such as good communication skills, broad knowledge base, empathy and sensitivity, ability to prioritise and work in a team) and used this as a basis to design a process to identify people with those skills. It is not difficult to imagine what the selectors choosing potential trainees in O&G might be looking for. All the attributes described above would be desirable combined with high degree of enthusiasm and interest in the clinical aspects of the actual work. A degree of realism is useful however; good candidates will be able to demonstrate that they have taken steps to find out more about what they are getting into and are aware of the nature of the job at the end of the training. All of us recognise that O&G is a demanding speciality in terms of out-of-hours commitment and we are concerned to try and ensure that the people we appoint will have the stamina to stay the course and complete training.

The application process at the time of writing is run centrally by the Royal College of Obstetricians and Gynaecologists (RCOG)

via a link from the College website and the timings relating to submitting your forms and the interviews can be found there: www.obsjobs.rcog.org.uk

There is usually a high degree of anxiety amongst candidates about filling in the form. Application forms for selection into the Foundation Programme and specialty training may seem like an exercise in creative writing (rather like the personal statement you wrote for selection into medical school). If you can put yourself into the shoes of the selectors and think "what are they looking for here?" for each section, it will help you to devise a high scoring response.

There is a big difference between this selection process and the Foundation Programme: you will have realised by now that you are on the job market and your application form must be taken more seriously. Most UK graduates will get a place on the Foundation Programme because we have to ensure that you are able to register with the General Medical Council and F1 is regarded as an extension of medical school – the consequences if your application does not score very highly are merely that you might not get the Foundation rotation that you wanted. The stakes are much higher than that now as this is about your future career and competition is fierce. I expect that you are consulting publications such as this in order to try and give yourself an edge over other candidates; a laudable aim. My aim as a selector is to try to choose candidates that appear to be trainable as obstetricians and gynaecologists.

You might have always known that you wanted to pursue a career in Obstetrics and Gynaecology, in which case you may have a slight advantage when it comes to filling in the application form because you will have been thinking about applying for O&G whilst you were still at medical school. You have probably already collected material that you could use as evidence on your application form.

If you selected Obstetrics and Gynaecology as one of the posts in your Foundation Programme as an experiment to see if you enjoy working in the specialty, then you need to do the post during your first Foundation year (F1) or during the first four-month slot of your second (F2) year. You will be filling in your application form before Christmas in F2 and most likely going for interview during the first three months of the following year, so you won't have experienced O&G unless it is your first F2 post. It might be difficult to arrange your rotation so that O&G is your first post, especially if there is someone else on your rotation wishing to do the same thing. If you know which hospital you are going to for F2, I would recommend that you discuss your F2 rotation with the administrator and the Foundation Programme Director of that Trust as early as possible before they have sorted out the order of rotation for the following year.

Don't worry if you have not done O&G since medical school as this will not affect your application. You might not have wanted or been able to get a rotation containing O&G during your Foundation Programme but this does not matter when it comes to applying for specialty training. We do not expect applicants to have had prior experience of O&G when they start at ST1, and it is just as valuable to have had training in other specialities where there is an obvious clinical overlap such as surgery, urology, paediatrics, psychiatry and anaesthetics. You will have had clinical experiences and acquired skills that will eventually prove useful to you at some point in your career and you will be able to draw on them and use some as examples when it comes to filling in the application form. They do not have to be related to O&G at all.

The entry criteria for all levels of application are strictly adhered to during short listing. If you are applying at ST1 for example, having more than 18 months experience in O&G will exclude you from consideration even if it was in a very different, possibly non-training post overseas. There is no point in wasting your chance by applying at ST1; you will have to apply at ST2 level even if there are fewer posts available.

If you are not currently in the UK Foundation Programme you will also need to supply evidence that you have attained 'Foundation competencies' if you are applying at ST1; do not leave the boxes for this evidence blank or your application will not be considered. The aim of the UK Foundation Programme is to produce doctors who have enough knowledge to manage emergency situations safely. If you are not sure what is involved in 'Foundation competencies' you can find the curriculum on the website at www.mmc

As you might imagine we insist on this because patient safety is paramount; for example we are keen to avoid a situation where we have employed a doctor who cannot safely resuscitate a collapsed patient with a ruptured ectopic pregnancy, because they are unable to obtain IV access.

Clinical knowledge and experience
If you are applying at ST1, you will be entering details of competencies you have attained in the Foundation Programme here. At higher levels of application, when you are talking about previous clinical experience and competencies within the specialty you should indicate the level that you are currently at i.e. performing the procedure under direct supervision or able to do the procedure without supervision.

On behalf of the RCOG, the panel considers that assessing your level of competence is crucial if you are applying at ST3 level. The transition from ST2 to ST3 is an important one in our speciality as most trainees in ST3 are working at 'registrar' level i.e. you will be responsible for looking after the labour ward and will have to deal with gynaecological emergencies such as ruptured ectopic pregnancy. In many hospitals you may be the most senior person on site working with a consultant on call from home, so it would be inappropriate and clinically dangerous to put a trainee into this role who could not do the job e.g. perform a caesarean section unsupervised in an emergency situation such as cord prolapse. If a trainee at ST2 in run-through training is not ready to work at this level, they may be asked to spend more time in ST2 before progressing to ST3 within the training programme; so it is important to impress on the selection panel that you can function safely at this level. You only have 100 words in which to sell yourself, so you will need to be concise.

Your training priorities for the next 12 months constitute your personal development plan that you will try to follow if you are appointed. It is sensible to try and put together a series of targets that are achievable and appropriate to your level of training; for example we would not expect a trainee coming in to a programme at ST3 level to state that they wish to learn advanced fertility techniques to prepare themselves for a glittering career in IVF. It would be sensible if to include specific details in your plan such as courses you might wish to go on, studies or audits you might want to continue or initiate, or procedures you wish to learn. This box on the form is not there for you to demonstrate what you already know; that sort of information should go into the experience box above and again, you only have 100 words. If you are not sure what sort of thing you should be learning at the level of training you are applying for, you will find more detail on the RCOG website www.rcog.org.uk

Extracurricular activities and achievements relevant to a career in O&G

Describing extracurricular activities and achievements can and should be used to demonstrate what sort of person you are, and perhaps to show that you have leadership potential – something we are looking for in our future consultants. You might wish to use something you did in the community such as youth work or voluntary work previously or perhaps something you did at medical school that shows you are prepared to get involved in activities outside medicine. Activities that fit the bill here may be sport-related, educational or social and don't feel embarrassed to go back as far as school if there is something relevant such as being a prefect. I suggest that you include something that you are proud of and can describe enthusiastically; we will be more impressed with your answer if you can describe how it has changed or developed you as a person that makes you ideal for selection into our speciality.

Audit, management, information technology
It is important to use personal experience if you are asked about audit as you may be asked about it in the interview. For example in the 2009 application form there are 200 words for describing your involvement with audit and you are asked to use a maximum of two audits to illustrate. Answers that include evidence of closure of the audit loop and a description of clinical changes that were made in the hospital as a result will naturally score higher than those where the audit is merely described. Don't forget to describe exactly what you did to contribute towards the project as we will be awarding marks for that, too.

You could use an example from outside medicine to describe your experience of teamwork if you have something that fits better than a clinical example. The nature of the experience does not matter as long as your description clearly demonstrates your role in the team and what happened as a result. The same thing applies to the question about management roles; what we are looking for is leadership potential and a willingness to involve yourself in organising things. Do not just describe the role; we are more interested in its effect on you, so tell us what you did and how it developed you as a person.

There cannot be many people who have not had some involvement in IT systems in this day and age. Even if you have not actually done a formal course e.g. the European computer driving license, you have probably used a computer for something related to medicine or education in the past. Try and be specific about what you can do with a computer.

Other achievements and personal skills

We are trying to discover something about your personality. It would be better to use something different from the extracurricular activity you described in the previous section and try to select something that shows that you have good communication skills. As well as describing an achievement outside medicine, you only have 150 words to convince the selection panel that you are well rounded, balanced person with a life outside medicine. You might describe what you do to relieve stress in your life, as we all recognise that we are in a stressful profession and we are hoping to select people who will be able to cope with awful things happening at work.

The scenario you choose to describe to illustrate problem solving and decision making should be clinical because it asks you about something that happened in the workplace. It will be easier to use prior clinical experience as examples if you have engaged in reflective practice during your previous posts e.g. in the Foundation Programme or as a medical student. Do answer the question and don't forget to describe how you personally dealt with it, as this will score more than just telling us what the situation was. This sort of question sometimes has a different focus e.g. describe how you dealt with a difficult ethical situation or functioned as a member of a team. The point of it is for the panel to see how you deal with things that go wrong in your work life and how thoughtful and resilient you are likely to be as a trainee.

Asking you about drive and initiative is aimed at measuring the amount of effort you are likely to put into your training. You could use examples from outside medicine to illustrate how you did something out of the ordinary or perhaps overcame difficulties in order to achieve something or had to find a way round a problem in your personal or professional life. They key thing is to describe the effect on you and how you coped – it is asking you to illustrate your drive, not just to describe the situation.

Academic achievements

If you do have publications, please do use the Vancouver style as requested. We may check up on references cited here, so be aware of that and do not be tempted to put in papers that you have not yet had accepted – they will be ignored. Entering your name in capitals on the reference removes the anonymity from the application form, but the reason for asking you to do that is so that we can see if you are the first author or not.

Many of you will have had teaching experience at medical school or in previous posts and if you have received positive feedback from the recipients you should try and mention that somewhere in the limited number of words that you are allowed. If you have received any formal training for delivering teaching, this will score extra points so don't forget to describe that.

Commitment to specialty

We are looking for people who have a realistic view of what they can expect from a career in O&G and some knowledge of how they are going to get there. If you are interested in a career in O&G but have no idea of which area might attract you in the long term, there is no problem with saying that on your form: many people only decide on a career path once they have had a chance to sample different aspects of the work. My suggestion is that you should be frank in this part of the form and tell us what it is that makes you want to do this for a career. Your reasons for applying for this particular programme may be geographical (i.e. you wish to train in the area where your family lives or your partner is employed) or it may be the training opportunities within that particular deanery that attract you, for example you may be able to rotate through tertiary referral centres or get access to academic posts or research opportunities. Perhaps you have had prior experience of the hospitals in the area as a student or in previous posts. I would recommend that you spend some time finding out more about the deanery that you have applied to; both the geography (i.e. the hospitals that you may rotate to) and the actual training available before you answer that part of the question.

Learning and personal development
Describing your attitude to learning and developing yourself as a person helps us get some measure of your personality and the chances of you having the stamina to continue through many years of academic and practical learning in this specialty. Obviously the people reading and assessing your application form think that it is worth the effort; they have all done this before you. Your reply should convince them that you are one of them and that you will be able to use a regularly updated personal development plan to ensure that you get to the end of the training programme with the skill set required to be a consultant in O&G in the UK.

As you are filling out your application form, you might find yourself asking if you are really sure that you want to do O&G for the rest of your life and the form may make you reconsider your career plans. Luckily there are plenty of sources of careers advice.

If you are having trouble making your career decision there is usually a plethora of careers advice available to you during the Foundation Programme such as careers fairs, meetings and study days and it is up to you to avail yourself of these facilities. It is possible that your local obstetricians and gynaecologists will organise O&G-specific events which you should attend if possible because you are likely to pick up ideas and phrases to use in your application form, especially when you hear people in the specialty talking about why they chose to go into O&G. It is possible that these will also be the people reading and scoring your application form, as enthusiastic clinicians who are prepared to give up their own time to speak at one of these events are likely to be the people involved in the selection and education of the next generation.

During Foundation you are entitled to take so-called 'taster days' which are designed to assist you with your career choice. Again, you might want to consider accessing taster days early in case you want to use any of the clinical experiences you acquire during these on your application form.

There are other sources of advice, such as your educational and clinical supervisors during the Foundation Programme and I would also recommend that you talk to doctors already working in the speciality such as SpRs, Staff grade and Associate Specialist doctors to find out what the job is really about.

The College may be able to help you with your career decision. As you might imagine the RCOG is keen to encourage recruitment into the specialty and usually runs an annual careers fair on a Saturday in the autumn which is free to attend (although it necessitates travelling to London). You can also register on the College website as an interested student or trainee free of charge and get access to information that will help you decide on your career path.

I should reiterate that when you are filling in your application forms, the score for each section will be enhanced if you can explain how and why the example that you are using illustrates the point. It is tempting to describe a scenario which may interest the selectors, but it will not score highly unless you have explained how it demonstrates that you personally have the attribute they are looking for. Make sure that you answer the whole question. If you are asked describe a situation when you have worked as part of a team, for example, you might spend most of your mental energy trying to decide which scenario to choose that best describes teamwork. Having chosen an entirely appropriate scenario, if you then just describe the clinical aspects and completely forget to write about your role in the team and how you contributed to the success of the team, your answer will unnecessarily lose marks.

You might have got the message by now that planning for your application starts early – preferably before you have left medical school. This might seem rather too early to be thinking about speciality training but when you understand what we are looking for, it all becomes rather obvious and I hope that you will have already started collecting portfolio items to impress the panel of assessors whilst you are still at medical school. I usually advise students who are intending to pursue a career in O&G to engage fully with everything that happens in the department, to spend extra time on the labour ward so that they can get a lot of practical experience, get involved in audits, look actively for suitable clinical material for case presentations, attend any postgraduate meetings that are going on and possibly enter the RCOG student prize competition. This sort of thing will impress the panel that you have an intense interest in the speciality and will give you examples to use to explain your motivation. If you have discussed your career with O&G doctors or gone out of your way to find out about it, such as attending careers fairs or using taster days it will be easier for you to explain how you have developed your understanding and insight into the speciality.

You may be asked to demonstrate that your skills and attributes are suitable for a career in O&G and this will be difficult to answer unless you have given it some thought during the time you have spent in the specialty during medical school and / or the Foundation Programme. You might have discovered that you have a talent for surgery or perhaps you found the excitement of working on the labour ward to your taste. Examples that you give to support your evidence will score higher marks from the panel if you can explain why they are relevant; try and imagine what the assessors are looking for in any particular part of the application form. For example, if there is a question about your motivation the assessors will be looking for a high degree of commitment but also some realism from candidates in the form of comments which show that you really know what working in O&G is like (for example, obstetrics by its very nature involves a heavy emphasis on unsocial hours and fairly onerous on call duties).

You might be asked to provide evidence of activities or achievements over and above your regular scheduled daily activities that demonstrate your commitment to the speciality or show that you have developed relevant skills. The sort of evidence that fits in here might be a project you did as part of your student elective or a special study module, a case report you presented or wrote up or participation in an audit. If you are going to use something like this it is important to validate it with dates and venues relating to the evidence if you can e.g. the hospital audit meeting at which your audit was presented.

Your reflective learning experiences as a student or during Foundation may help you answer clinical questions such as using your clinical judgement to make a significant impact on a patient, thinking "outside the box" to solve a clinical problem, working under pressure or discussing a sensitive issue with a patient. Examples that you use to illustrate these answers should only be used once on your application form; it impresses the panel much less if the same clinical scenario turns up in every answer.

On a practical note, each section has a limited character count and it can be difficult to construct your responses so that you can get all you want to say in the small amount of space available. I would advise that you 'cut and paste' your answers and work on them for some time, including doing a careful character count with spelling and grammar check. I would also recommend that you do not leave this until the last minute so that you have got time to re-read and possibly re-word your answers a few days after you have composed the original text. Your responses often seem different when you look at your application form again and you may want to change the wording several times before finally pressing the button to submit it. A second or even third look is always valuable.

Good luck!

Chapter 2
The Royal College of Obstetricians & Gynaecologists ObsJobs Website

By Matthew Huggins, Deputy Head of Postgraduate Training,
The Royal College of Obstetricians & Gynaecologists

If you are interested in a career in obstetrics and gynaecology, one of your first ports of call should be the ObsJobs website, which can be found at https://obsjobs.rcog.org.uk/. The site was developed by the Royal College of Obstetricians and Gynaecologists (RCOG) in 2007. It has now been used for the harmonised recruitment rounds that took place in 2008, 2009 and the ongoing round taking place in 2010. It has proved to be very successful, with deaneries filling 100% of the specialty training (ST) posts on offer in 2009.

The harmonised recruitment process devised by the RCOG involves all deaneries in England and Wales and was designed to make it easier for applicants to apply for training posts. Applicants apply via the online application form, having first ranked all deaneries to which they wish to apply. Much more detailed information about the process can be found in the FAQ document available on the ObsJobs website [https://obsjobs.rcog.org.uk/info/general_info]. The website also contains person specifications, example application forms, interview dates and other helpful information.

Generally, there are two recruitment periods per year. The main round commences in December (for posts commencing the following August) and the smaller second round takes place in the autumn (for posts commencing the following February). There are usually between 350 and 400 ST/FTSTA/LAT posts available during the main recruitment period and around 10 ST posts available in the second round.

For the latest news on recruitment, please visit https://obsjobs.rcog.org.uk/

Chapter 3
Person Specification

These are self explanatory, the person specification for ST1.

2010 Person Specification		
Application to enter Specialty Training at ST1: Obstetrics & Gynaecology		
Entry Criteria		
	Essential	**When Evaluated[1]**
Qualifications	MBBS or equivalent medical qualification	Application form
Eligibility	• Eligible for full registration with the GMC at time of appointment and hold a current licence to practice.[2]	Application form
	• Evidence of achievement of Foundation competences between 31st July 2007 and 4th August 2010 from a UKFPO affiliated Foundation Programme or equivalent by time of appointment in line with GMC standards/ Good Medical Practice including: :	Application form Interview / Selection centre[3]
	o Good clinical care o Maintaining good medical practice o Good relationships and communication with patients o Good working relationships with colleagues o Good teaching and training o Professional behaviour and probity o Delivery of good acute clinical care	
	(Details of the specific competences are detailed within the Foundation Learning Portfolio, one of several relevant documents available for download at: http://www.foundationprogramme.nhs.uk/pages/home/key-documents)	Application form
	• Eligibility to work in the UK	
Fitness To Practise	Is up to date and fit to practise safely	Application form References
Language Skills	All applicants to have demonstrable skills in written and spoken English adequate to enable effective communication about medical topics with patients and colleagues demonstrated by one of the following:	Application form Interview / Selection centre
	o that applicants have undertaken undergraduate medical training in English; or	
	o have achieved the following scores in the academic International English Language Testing System (IELTS) in a single sitting within 24 months at time of application – Overall 7, Speaking 7, Listening 7, Reading 7, Writing 7.	
	If applicants believe they have adequate communication skills but do not fit into one of these examples they must provide supporting evidence	
Health	Meets professional health requirements (in line with GMC standards/ Good Medical Practice)	Application form Pre-employment health screening
Career Progression	• Ability to provide a complete employment history	Application form
	• Evidence that career progression is consistent with personal circumstances	
	• Evidence that present achievement and performance is commensurate with totality of period of training	
	• 18 months or less experience[4] in this specialty (not including Foundation modules) by August 2010	

---

[1] 'when evaluated' is indicative, but may be carried out at any time throughout the selection process
[2] The GMC will introduce a licence to practice in the autumn of 2009. Any doctor wishing to practice in the UK after this date must be both registered and hold a licence to practice.
[3] A selection centre is a process not a place. It involves a number of selection activities that may be delivered within the Unit of Application.
[3] Any time periods specified in this person specification refer to full time equivalent
[4] All experience in posts at ST level count irrespective of the country the experience is gained in

© The Royal College of Obstetricians and Gynaecologists

Application Completion	**ALL** sections of application form completed **FULLY** according to written guidelines	Application form

Selection Criteria			
	Essential	**Desirable**	**When Evaluated**
Qualifications	As above	• Intercalated BSc, BA, MSc involving time taken out from standard five year undergraduate medical curriculum. • MD or PhD (Note: will only score if awarded for defending a thesis; **_not_** for primary or secondary medical degree. This usually equates to 2-3 years spent in pure research with minimal clinical activity)	Application form Interview / Selection centre
Clinical Experience, Training & Skills	• Evidence of successful completion of Basic Life Support course or equivalent, in the 12 months prior to submitting an application • Awareness of own training needs	• Shows aptitude for practical skills, e.g. manual dexterity • Relevant experience in other specialties which would complement a career in obstetrics & gynaecology • Extracurricular activities / achievements relevant to obstetrics & gynaecology	Application form Interview / Selection centre References
Academic / Research Skills	• Demonstrates understanding of the basic principles of research • Experience of active involvement in Audit (clear description, outcomes & appropriate experience for level of application)	• Formal academic achievement is not a pre-requisite for application to obstetrics and gynaecology at ST1 level, but *relevant* achievements will be considered as part of the overall assessment of an application	Application form
Awards And Prizes		Evidence of: • Other relevant degrees or diplomas • Academic prizes and honours *at undergraduate or postgraduate level*	Application form Interview / Selection centre

Personal Skills	**Communication Skills:**		Application form
	• Capacity to communicate effectively		Interview / Selection centre
	Empathy & Sensitivity:		References
	• Capacity to take in others' perspectives and treat others with understanding		
	Managing Others & Team Involvement:		
	• Contribution to team work (may be within or out with the working environment)		
	Problem Solving & Decision Making:		
	• Demonstrates problem-solving, decision-making & situational awareness		
	Organisation & Planning:		
	• Relevant contribution to management *within or out with* the working environment (rotas, committees etc)		
	• IT skills		
	Coping with Pressure:		
	• Capacity to manage acute situations under pressure		
	• Demonstrates initiative & resilience to cope with changing circumstances		
Probity	**Professional Integrity & Respect for Others:**		Application form
	• Clearly demonstrates drive and initiative		Interview / Selection centre
	• Capacity to take responsibility for own actions and demonstrate a non-judgemental approach towards others		References
	• Displays honesty, integrity, awareness of confidentiality & ethical issues		
Commitment To Specialty	**Learning & Personal Development:**		Application form
	• Demonstrates realistic insight into obstetrics & gynaecology as practiced in the UK	• Extracurricular activities / achievements relevant to obstetrics & gynaecology	Interview / Selection centre
	• Commitment to personal and professional development, including capacity for reflective practice & learning		References
	• Sound reasons for applying to this particular post		

Chapter 4
The Application Form

The one shown here is for a ST1 application, the ST2 & ST3 are very similar. The application process is online. As a precaution against accidental loss of your data, it is a good idea to prepare your answers in a Word document, which will give you the added opportunity to spell-check and count your words before pasting them into your application form.

1.4

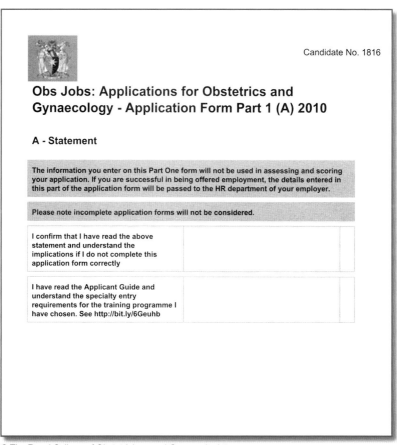

Candidate No. 1816

Obs Jobs: Applications for Obstetrics and Gynaecology - Application Form Part 1 (A) 2010

A - Statement

The information you enter on this Part One form will not be used in assessing and scoring your application. If you are successful in being offered employment, the details entered in this part of the application form will be passed to the HR department of your employer.

Please note incomplete application forms will not be considered.

I confirm that I have read the above statement and understand the implications if I do not complete this application form correctly	
I have read the Applicant Guide and understand the specialty entry requirements for the training programme I have chosen. See http://bit.ly/6Geuhb	

B - Personal Details

Surname/Family Name	
First Names	
Name in which you are registered with the GMC if different to above	
Title	
Date of Birth	
UK National Insurance Number	
Contact Address	
Postcode	
Country	
Home Telephone	
Mobile Telephone	
Work Telephone	
May we contact you at work?	
Email address - please note most recruitment communications will be via email so you must provide an active email address which you check regularly. You must inform the recruiting deanery of any change.	
See advice in the Applicant Guide concerning the best email addresses to use in your application form.	
If you have a disability do you require any specific arrangements to enable you to attend for interview?	
If yes, please supply details below	

© The Royal College of Obstetricians and Gynaecologists

If you have a disability, provided you meet the minimum criteria as specified in the Person Specification, do you wish to be considered under the Guaranteed Interview Scheme? Please see the Disability Discrimination Act for more details	
Do you wish to apply for a deferred start date because you are registered for a higher degree (e.g. PhD, MD)?	
Date available to start post (If this is later than August 2010 please give reasons):	
Do you wish to be considered for less than full-time training? If you select 'Yes' this information will not be made known to the selection panel but you will need to apply formally for less than full-time training via the deanery Flexible Training Team. Further guidance and details on how to apply can be found on the deanery website.	

C - Eligibility to Apply

Professional Registration	
Do you have, or are you eligible for, FULL registration with Licence to Practise awarded by the GMC at time of your appointment	
GMC Registration No.	
Date of FULL registration	
Renewal date	

D - Language Skills

You are required to demonstrate skills in written and spoken English that are adequate to enable effective communication about medical and/or health topics with patients, colleagues and the public.

Evidence of English language proficiency (please check all boxes that apply to you). If you select 'No' to both options then you must complete the 'Other' section.

Country of Primary Medical Qualification	
Was your undergraduate training taught in English?	
Have your language skills been tested through the IELTS (2) (International English Language Testing System) to the minimum overall score required as per the Person Specification (3)?	
Overall Score	
Speaking Score	
Listening Score	
Reading Score	
Writing Score	
Date IELTS taken	
Other – please provide details below – provide evidence of your English language proficiency	

(2) See advice in the Applicant Guide for more information on the IELTS test

(3) The Applicant must have achieved as a minimum the following scores in the academic International English Language Testing System (IELTS) in a single sitting within 24 months at time of application – Overall 7, Speaking 7, Listening 7, Reading 7, Writing 7

© The Royal College of Obstetricians and Gynaecologists

E - Right to Work in the United Kingdom

Your eligibility to apply for this position will be determined by your immigration status on the closing date for applications for this post. Some applicants may be considered before others on the basis of immigration status, in accordance with the Immigration, Asylum and Nationality Act 2006.

If you are shortlisted, you will be required to produce the original documents (passports, page with the stamp and letter from the Home Office) on the interview day.

Are you a United Kingdom (UK), European Community (EC) or European Economic Area (EEA) national?	
If not, do you have evidence of entitlement to enter and work permanently in the United Kingdom (i.e. Indefinite Leave to Remain – free from immigration control?)	
Are you on a dependents visa (If you have answered YES please complete the Partner/Civil Partner/Spouse status section)	

If you have selected no to both of the above please select 'Yes' from the drop down lists below when appropriate and complete start and expiry date of your permit:

Personal Status

Nationality	

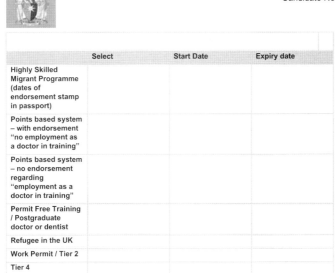

	Select	Start Date	Expiry date
Highly Skilled Migrant Programme (dates of endorsement stamp in passport)			
Points based system – with endorsement "no employment as a doctor in training"			
Points based system – no endorsement regarding "employment as a doctor in training"			
Permit Free Training / Postgraduate doctor or dentist			
Refugee in the UK			
Work Permit / Tier 2			
Tier 4			
UK ancestry			
Student visa holder			
Other immigration categories i.e. Overseas government employees, Innovators etc			

If Other than above, please specify the immigration category	

Partner / civil partner / spouse status.

Please complete this section if you have answered YES to question "Are you on a dependents visa" above.

	Select	Start Date	Expiry Date
Partner / civil partner or spouse of UK / EEA citizen			
Non EEA national partner / civil partner or spouse of EEA citizen exercising a treaty right			
Points based system – no endorsement regarding "employment as a doctor in training"			
Partner / civil partner or spouse under the Points based system – with endorsement "no employment as a doctor in training"			
Partner / civil partner or spouse under the Points based system – no endorsement regarding "employment as a doctor in training"			
Partner / civil partner or spouse of student visa holder – student visa holder must have 12 months or more leave to remain			
Partner / civil partner or spouse of other immigration categories i.e. refugees, work permit holders, Overseas government employees, Innovators etc.			
If Other than above, please specify the immigration category			

If you are shortlisted, you will be required to produce the original documents (passports, page with the stamp and letter from the Home Office) on the interview day.

F - Fitness to Practise

It is vitally important that you read, understand and answer all the questions asked in this section. Please read the notes below carefully before completing this part of the form.

This post is considered a "regulated activity" within the terms of the Safeguarding Vulnerable Groups Act 2006, and appointments made after 26 July 2010 will be subject to registration with the Independent Safeguarding Authority (ISA)

We aim to promote equality of opportunity and are committed to treating all applicants for positions fairly and on merit regardless of race, gender, marital status, religion, disability, sexual orientation or age. We undertake not to discriminate unfairly against applicants on the basis of criminal conviction or other information declared.

Prior to making a final decision concerning your application, we shall discuss with you any information declared by you that we believe may have a bearing on your suitability for the position. If we do not raise this information with you, this is because we do not believe that it should be taken into account. In that event, you still remain free, should you wish to discuss the matter with the interviewing panel. As part of assessing your application, we will only take into account relevant criminal record and other information declared.

The Data Protection Act 1998 requires us to provide you with certain information and to obtain your consent before processing sensitive data about you. Processing includes: obtaining, recording, holding, disclosing, destruction and retaining information. Sensitive personal data includes any of the following information: criminal offences, criminal convictions, criminal proceedings, disposal or sentence, registration status with the Independent Safeguarding Authority (from 26 July 2010).

The information that you provide in this Declaration Form will be processed in accordance with the Data Protection Act 1998. It will be used for the purpose of determining your application for this position. It will also be used for purposes of enquiries in relation to the prevention and detection of fraud. Once a decision has been made concerning your appointment, we will not retain this Declaration Form longer than is necessary (ie until you leave the post you are applying for / programme or the recruitment episode is closed).

This Declaration Form and any information provided relating to a positive declaration will be kept securely and in confidence, and access to it will be restricted to designated persons within the Recruitment Department and other persons who need to see it as part of the selection process and who are authorised to do so. If successfully appointed to a training post, this information may be passed to your employing trusts.

Rehabilitation of Offenders Act 1974

Before you can be considered for appointment in a position of trust as a Specialty Trainee on a Deanery programme, we need to be satisfied about your character and suitability.

This post is considered a "regulated activity" within the terms of the Safeguarding Vulnerable Groups Act 2006, and appointments made after 26 July 2010 will be subject to registration with the Independent Safeguarding Authority (ISA). This will become a mandated requirement from 1st November 2010. Only successfully registered employees will be permitted to continue their training and employment after that date.

The post is also exempted from the Rehabilitation of Offenders Act 1974. This means that you must declare all criminal convictions, including those that would otherwise be considered "spent".

Answering "YES" to any of the questions below will not necessarily bar you from appointment. This will depend on the nature of the position for which you are applying and the particular circumstances.

Please answer all of the following questions. If you answer "YES" to any of the questions, please provide full details on a separate sheet of paper and place in a sealed envelope addressed to the deanery. Alternatively, you can email the details to the deanery. Please mark the envelope "CONFIDENTIAL".

If you would like to discuss what effect any previous convictions, police investigations or fitness to practise proceedings taken or being taken either in the UK or by an overseas licensing or regulatory body might have on your application, you may telephone the deanery.

Are you currently bound over or have you ever been convicted of any offence by a Court or Court-Martial in the United Kingdom or in any other country? NB: You do not need to tell us about parking offences.	
Have you ever received a police caution, reprimand or final warning?	
Have you been charged with any offence in the United Kingdom or in any other country that has not yet been disposed of? Please note: You are reminded that if you are appointed to a training post or programme, you will have a continuing responsibility to inform your employer(s) and the Postgraduate Dean of any new criminal convictions, police investigations or fitness to practise proceedings that arise in the future. You do not need to tell us if you are charged with a parking offence.	

© The Royal College of Obstetricians and Gynaecologists

Are you aware of any current police investigation in the United Kingdom or in any other country following allegations made against you?

Are you aware of any current NHS Counter Fraud and Security Management Service (CFSMS) investigation following allegations made against you?

Have you ever been investigated by the Police, CFSMS or any other Investigatory Body resulting in a caution, conviction or dismissal from your employment? (Investigatory bodies include Local Authorities, Customs & Excise, Immigration, Passport Agency, Inland Revenue, Department of Trade & Industry, Banks and Building Societies, General Life Insurance Companies – this list is not exhaustive, and you must declare any investigation conducted by an Investigatory Body).

Have you ever been dismissed by reason of misconduct from any employment, office or other position previously held by you?

Have you ever been disqualified from the practice of a profession or required to practice subject to specified limitations / conditions / warnings following fitness to practise proceedings by a regulatory or licensing body in the United Kingdom or in any other country?

Are you currently the subject of any investigation or fitness to practice proceeding by any employer, any licensing or regulatory body in the United Kingdom or any other country?

Are you subject to any other prohibition, limitation, or restriction that means we are unable to consider you for the position for which you are applying?

G - References

Reference reports are not used for scoring purposes during shortlisting or interview but will be reviewed during the selection process and again prior to confirmation of appointment for successful applicants. The reference process is designed to check the accuracy of your previous employment and training history and to provide assurance of your qualifications, integrity and track record.

You must provide contact details, including e-mail addresses, of three referees who have supervised your clinical training during the last two years of your employment or undergraduate training. One referee must be your current or most recent consultant or educational supervisor familiar with your clinical development.

Your clinical referees should be contacted by you in advance to confirm that they are willing to provide a reference and are available and able to do so in the time period required for selection and appointment, should you be successful.

Please ensure these details are correct as you will be unable to begin in post until references are supplied and checked.

Employment or Training Post 1 : This Clinical Referee must be your present or most recent Consultant or Educational Supervisor

Specialty	
Training Grade	
Start Date	
End Date	
Name of Consultant or educational supervisor	
Job Title	
In what capacity did they work with you?	
Contact email address	
Contact postal address	
Phone number(1) Switchboard (2) Direct Dial	

© The Royal College of Obstetricians and Gynaecologists

Fax number (where applicable)

Employment or Training Post 2

Specialty

Training Grade

Start Date

End Date

Name of Consultant or GP supervisor

Job Title

In what capacity did they work with you?

Contact email address

Contact postal address

Phone number(1) Switchboard (2) Direct Dial

Fax number (where applicable)

Employment or Training Post 3

Specialty

Training Grade

Start Date

End Date

Name of Consultant or GP supervisor

Job Title

In what capacity did they work with you?

Contact email address		
Contact postal address		
Phone number(1) Switchboard (2) Direct Dial		
Fax number (where applicable)		

© The Royal College of Obstetricians and Gynaecologists

H - Entry Criteria checklist

You should tick the following checklist to indicate that you have completed this application form in conjunction with the entry criteria set out in the relevant Specialty/entry level Person Specification for the post applied for.

I meet the essential qualifications

I have the right to work in the UK

I hold a current GMC Licence to Practise

I have no fitness to practise restrictions, or any other prohibition, limitation or restriction which would prevent me from applying for this post

I am proficient in English Language Skills at the required level

I am aware of the recruitment arrangements for my chosen specialty and entry level contained in the Applicant Guide http://www.rcog.org.uk/

Obs Jobs: Applications for Obstetrics and Gynaecology - Application Form Part 2 (B) 2010 Obs Jobs

Section A – Professional qualifications

Medical School/University	
Start Date	

Shortlisted candidates will be required to bring original certificates to the interviews

Basic Medical Degree	
Awarding Body	
Country of Qualification	
Date of Qualification	

Other degrees completed during undergraduate medical training - you must only list other degrees (eg BSc, BA, etc) if this required formal time to be taken out of the undergraduate medical curriculum.

Degree & Class	Awarding Body	Date of Qualification

Other degrees or diplomas - including higher (postgraduate) degrees - Complete ALL sections. You must only list a PhD or MD in this section which has been awarded for defending a thesis, and fulfils the following criteria - Not a primary or secondary medical degree, and an additional 2-3 years of dedicated postgraduate study without the candidate being employed in a regular clinical post.

Degree / Diploma / Class	Country	Awarding Body	Date of Qualification
For postgraduate degree (PhD or MD) as defined above, please enter the title of your thesis			
Prizes or awards at academic level			

1.4

Section B - Entry Criteria

By August 2010 how many months experience (at SHO level or equivalent) in Obstetrics & Gynaecology will you have? (DO NOT include time spent in Foundation modules)	
During your Foundation Programme, how much time did you spend in Obstetrics & Gynaecology or related specialties?	
I confirm that I will have no more than 18 months (whole time equivalent) experience in Obstetrics and Gynaecology (not including Foundation modules), in the UK and overseas, by August 2010.	

Achievement of Foundation Competences

Have you been issued with a Certificate of Completion of Foundation Training?	
If 'No', do you expect to be issued with a Certificate of Completion of Foundation Training by August 2010?	
If not applying directly from Foundation Training, have you gained Foundation competences?	

If not applying directly from Foundation Training, please indicate what evidence you will provide to demonstrate that you have gained Foundation competences. Choose all that apply:

Portfolio evidence of achievement of competences	
Checklist of competences achieved, countersigned by trainer	
Evidence of having completed educationally-approved SHO post(s) in the UK	
Other – please specify below	

© The Royal College of Obstetricians and Gynaecologists

Other evidence of achievement of Foundation competences (only complete this if you have selected 'Other' above).		

C(1) - Present Employment

Employer's name	
Address	
Telephone number	

Current/Most Recent Position

Specialty	Grade (if relevant, state if LAT/LAS)	Date appointed	Length of contract	Length of notice required in weeks

C(2) - Previous Appointments in Obstetrics and Gynaecology

Please list posts in chronological order and state if locum/temporary/substantive posts.
DO NOT INCLUDE FOUNDATION MODULES.

Specialty, Hospital, Consultant	Grade (Substantive / Temporary / LAT / LAS)	From	To	Months in post

D - Previous Appointments in Other Specialties

Please list posts in chronological order and state if locum/temporary/substantive posts.
DO NOT INCLUDE FOUNDATION MODULES.

Specialty, Hospital, Consultant	Grade (Substantive / Temporary / LAT / LAS)	From	To	Months in Post
Do you have any gaps in your employment history of more than 4 weeks duration?				
If 'Yes', please explain the gap and give relevant dates.				

E(1) - Clinical Knowledge and Experience

Please give details of your clinical experience and level of competence. Do not list numbers of specific procedures.	
If you were to be appointed, what would your training priorities be in your next 12 month post?	

E(2) - Extracurricular activities/achievements relevant to a career in O&G

Please give details of any additional extracurricular activities or achievements that you feel are relevant to a career in obstetrics and gynaecology.	
Have you completed training in Basic Life Support?	
Please give specific details (Essential for ALL applicants) - Date/Venue	

© The Royal College of Obstetricians and Gynaecologists

F - Audit, Management, Information Technology

Please describe your experience of clinical audit. Indicate clearly your own level of involvement. Describe any effects on clinical practice using no more than 2 example from your own audit experience.	
Please describe any experience of working closely with other people. You may give an example(s) from both inside and outside medicine.	
Describe any management roles you have been involved in at work (rota organizer, committees etc), or outside of medicine.	
Indicate your level of familiarity with Information Technology, and in particular note any formal qualifications.	

G - Other Achievements & Personal Skills

A range of personal skills have been identified as being particularly important in successful medical specialists. For each of the skills indicated below, please give an example, preferably recent, from your own experience, to illustrate how you dealt with particular situations. Unless specified, you may draw from work or from other outside activities.

COMMUNICATION AND INTERPERSONAL SKILLS. (i) What have you achieved outside of medicine and (ii) how do you balance work, family and leisure time?

PROBLEM SOLVING & DECISION-MAKING. SITUATIONAL AWARENESS. Please describe the most challenging situation you have faced in the workplace and how you dealt with this.

DRIVE & INITIATIVE. Please give an example that best illustrates your drive and initiative.

© The Royal College of Obstetricians and Gynaecologists

H - Academic Achievements - Research and Teaching

Research, whether past or in progress. If you have undertaken or are undertaking a research project, please give details. Indicate your involvement, funding, source, length.	

Papers in peer-reviewed journals. Candidates will need to bring copies of all publications to interview. MAXIMUM 3 PUBLICATIONS. DO NOT INCLUDE CASE REPORTS OR ABSTRACTS. Will not be counted unless a full reference is supplied in Vancouver style - Please CAPITALISE your name.

	Details
1	
2	
3	

Other publications (case reports etc, but not abstracts or letters). MAXIMUM 2 PUBLICATIONS. Will not be counted unless a full reference is supplied in Vancouver style - Please CAPITALISE your name.

	Details
1	
2	

Presentations at international, national or regional (not local) meetings. MAXIMUM 2 PRESENTATIONS (Oral OR Poster).

	Details
1	
2	

Please describe your experience of teaching others, including different teaching methods, attendance at formal teaching courses. You may wish to use examples from outside medicine.	

© The Royal College of Obstetricians and Gynaecologists

I - Commitment to Specialty

How will this training programme and your previous training and experience, help you meet your career objectives?	
What are your reasons for applying to this training programme?	

J - Learning and Personal Development

How would you demonstrate your commitment to personal and professional development? How do you set yourself realistic goals?	

K - Notes

Children and Vulnerable Adults - Where the appointment involves substantial access to children and/or vulnerable adults, the appointment is subject to a police check. The Criminal Records Bureau will be asked to verify that you have no convictions and cautions or pending prosecutions, convictions, cautions and bind-over orders. This will include local police force records in addition to checks with the Police National Computer and the government department lists held by the Department of Health and Department for Education and Employment, where appropriate.

Declaration - If you are related to a member or Senior Officer/Manager of the Trusts involved in the training programme, you must disclose such a relationship. You are also required to declare any involvement, either directly or indirectly, with any firm, company or organisation which has a contract with Trusts involved in the training programme. Failure to declare any information on these matters may result in your application being rejected or, if it is discovered after appointment that such information has been withheld, then this may lead to dismissal. Please note canvassing of a Senior Officer/Manager shall disqualify an applicant. Please state any disclosure/declaration related to the above in the box below:

Disclosure/declaration (please give specific details):	

L - Equal Opportunities

NHS employers are committed to equal opportunities. No applicants will be discriminated against on the grounds of colour, race, ethnic origin, nationality, age, disability, gender, sexual orientation, marital status, religion, or politics.

I have noted the above information

M - Accepting an Appointment

You must take up any post, including a locum post, you have formally accepted unless the employer has adequate time to make other arrangements. (Good Medical Practice published by the GMC – 3rd edition, May 2001). Failure to comply with this requirement may result in a complaint to the GMC.

I have noted the above information	

N - Confirmation that information submitted is correct

I understand that employment offered in this training programme is subject to satisfactory medical clearance and subject to the information provided on the application form or any other document being correct. The information you provide will be checked. Inaccuracies may result in your application being rejected and in extreme cases may merit a referral to the General Medical Council. Any false or misleading information provided on this form or any other document may result in any employment being terminated.

The Data Protection Act 1998 requires us to provide you with certain information and to obtain your consent before processing data about you. Processing includes: obtaining, recording, holding, disclosing destruction and retaining information. The information that you provide on this application form will be processed in accordance with the Data Protection Act 1998, and will be used for recruitment and, if you are successful, will form part of your training record at the Deanery. If you are appointed, the information will be passed to your employing Trust. Information relating to your name, contact address, email address, date of birth, GMC/GDC registration, specialty, grade and your photograph will be passed to the Department of Health NHS Employers for the production of an Occupational Health Smartcard.

I understand and agree that the information provided on this form being entered onto the relevant Deanery(ies) computer information system and used for the Deanery(ies) legitimate business.

I confirm that I have read the Privacy information (at https://obsjobs.rcog.org.uk/info/privacy)		
I have noted the above information (note that by ticking this box, you are confirming that the information you have provided is correct and complete).		

Before submitting their application(s), candidates MUST check the relevant deanery website(s) for any additional information. PLEASE NOTE that the College is unable to provide copies of application forms after the relevant recruitment period is completed. Therefore candidates are advised to keep a copy of their application form(s).

© The Royal College of Obstetricians and Gynaecologists

Chapter 5
Competition Ratios

These will vary from year to year and are included for reference only.

Recruitment to Obstetrics and Gynaecology, 2010
Competition Ratios, 2009

This table shows the number of applications received per available post in the 2009 Recruitment Process for O&G (Round One only)

Deanery	Applications received at:			Posts available at:			Ratio of applications to posts at each level			
	ST1/ FTSTA1	ST2/ FTSTA2	ST3/ LAT	ST1/ FTSTA1	ST2/ FTSTA2	ST3/ LAT	ST1/ FTSTA1	ST2/ FTSTA2	ST3/ LAT	Overall
East Midlands - North	58	6	23	11	3	1	5.27	2.00	23.00	5.80
East Midlands - South	33	9	0	4	1	0	8.25	9.00	-	8.40
East of England	119	17	91	21	7	6	5.67	2.43	15.17	6.68
London-KSS	354	35	204	77	10	14	4.60	3.50	14.57	5.87
Mersey	75	0	0	12	0	0	6.25	-	-	6.25
North Western	136	0	4	19	0	1	7.16	-	4.00	7.00
Northern	78	3	32	14	2	5	5.57	1.50	6.40	5.38
Oxford	92	22	24	10	4	2	9.20	5.50	12.00	8.63
Severn	78	0	0	10	0	0	7.80	-	-	7.80
South West Peninsula	18	3	0	5	2	0	3.60	1.50	-	3.00
Wales	45	68	92	14	9	15	3.21	7.56	6.13	5.39
Wessex	63	16	35	10	4	4	6.30	4.00	8.75	6.33
West Midlands	142	38	128	22	8	5	6.45	4.75	25.60	8.80
Yorkshire and The Humber	150	82	59	25	9	3	6.00	9.11	19.67	7.86
Applications/posts per level:	1441	299	692	254	59	56			Overall ratio:	6.59
									Ratio in 2008:	7.12

Total applications received: 2432
Total posts available: 369

Please note that in 2010, East Midlands - North and East Midlands - South are one Unit of Application.
The figures for 'posts available' are taken from the number of posts that were available at the closing point for applications (23rd January 2009).

Chapter 6
Excerpts from past Applications

The following sections are mock examples are what strong candidates would write in these sections. They are fictional and serve only to give you an idea as to what extra curricular activities may score highly, any relation to actual applicants is unintentional.

Extra Curricular Activities

For my elective, I worked as an intern for UNICEF, Uganda on their Safe Motherhood Campaign. I was involved in an initiative to increase utilisation of maternal and neonatal health services. I produced a document, which I presented at a national meeting, on the barriers to achieving a reduction in maternal mortality in the 'developing' world. My dissertation on Female Genital Mutilation included an interview with Patricia Hewitt and was published in a book and came runner up in a competition for publication in The BJOG. I expect these achievements will be invaluable in a career in Obstetrics & Gynaecology.

Through my voluntary work I have demonstrated good situational awareness. I volunteered to help steward Christian events, the main event of the year being 'Celebration' with up to 20000 festival goers. My role was within a small team to help ensure festival safety, helping with queue management and searching for lost children. As a result of this I have completed a course on door-management, the Edexcel Level 2 BTEC Award in Door Supervision (June2005). This course taught me the skills needed to recognise and resolve difficult situations efficiently and effectively. All of which are essential for a career within obstetrics and gynaecology.

Working with other people

I was an organiser of a voluntary project over 6 months called 'Children's Allotment Project' in the final year of my training. The charity funded scheme involves securing an allotment and transforming it into a 'gardening after-school club' for the local school. I worked with a team of gardeners, school carers and volunteers. My role initially involved coordinating volunteers each weekend to prepare the allotment for the winter and spring seeding. Through phone calls and emails I ensured sufficient members were available to help with weeding. As the weather improved I planned with the school carers and gardeners to organise fun afternoons where my team and I would supervise children planting various fruits and vegetables and we would design teaching sessions on topics such as the water cycle. I learnt some gardening but more importantly the value of teamwork and allowing everyone to employ their talents.

Management Roles

As an avid Tango dancer I founded the University of Dublin Tango Dancing Society and remained the president of the society for three years. From bringing together several like-minded enthusiasts I formed a team dedicated to promoting tango dancing to the student population. I hired a professional Argentinean Tango teacher, co-ordinated venues for weekly lessons and social 'milonga' nights and oversaw the financial management. This often meant making difficult decisions and resolving conflicts between committee members to reach consensus. In the pre-'BBC Strictly Come Dancing' era we struggled not only with finances but persevered through many afternoons of advertising. As well as discovering a life-long interest my management skills, team play and leadership skills matured and I am very proud of the flourishing society today.

Chapter 7
Short listing score sheet

HARMONISED APPLICATION IN OBSTETRICS & GYNAECOLOGY – DECEMBER 2009
SHORT-LISTING SCORE SHEET – SPECIALTY TRAINING IN OBSTETRICS & GYNAECOLOGY – ST 1

PLEASE INSERT UNIQUE APPLICANT NUMBER HERE:

Advice for ST1 applicants - these sheets show the scoring system which will be used for short-listing from the application form. If the short-listing panel agrees that you have scored "0" in any of the essential criteria this means that you have not provided sufficient evidence to demonstrate the attribute. You therefore cannot be shortlisted. You are advised to self-assess yourself prior to application and to seek advice from your educational supervisor if necessary. **THIS SHOULD NOT BE RETURNED WITH YOUR APPLICATION. IT IS FOR YOUR INFORMATION ONLY.**

Scoring - where 'ranges' are used, the scoring equates to the following categories:-

- **Range '0 – 3'**   Achievement or Experience
  - 0 = 'none or minimal'
  - 1 = 'borderline'
  - 2 = 'average'
  - 3 = 'excellent, high quality, appropriate'

- **Range '0 – 2'**   Achievement or Experience
  - 0 = 'none or minimal'
  - 1 = 'moderate'
  - 2 = 'excellent'

ENTRY CRITERIA	Assessed In Section	YES/NO
MBBS (or equivalent)	Part 2, A	
Achievement of Foundation competencies by August 2010	Part 2, B	
A **maximum** of **18 months** experience in Obstetrics & Gynaecology (not including Foundation modules) by August 2010	Part 2, B	

ESSENTIAL CRITERIA	
Has this applicant scored a 0 in any of the essential criteria?	YES / NO
If an applicant scores 0 in any of the essential criteria, the application **must** be discussed at the shortlisting committee (or equivalent)	

© The Royal College of Obstetricians and Gynaecologists

ESSENTIAL CRITERIA

QUALIFICATIONS, AWARDS AND PRIZES – PART 2, SECTION A

ESSENTIAL CRITERIA	Max Score	Available Score	Applicant score

CLINICAL EXPERIENCE, TRAINING & SKILLS – PART 2, SECTIONS B - E

	Max Score	Available Score	Applicant score
Achieved appropriate competencies and clinical knowledge for application to ST1	3	(0 – 3)	
Awareness of own training needs	3	(0 – 3)	
Basic Life Support course	1	0 or 1	

ORGANISATION & PLANNING (AUDIT, MANAGEMENT, IT) – PART 2, SECTION F

	Max Score	Available Score	Applicant score
Experience of active involvement in Audit (clear description, outcomes & appropriate experience for level of application)	3	(0 – 3)	
Contribution to team work (may be within or outwith the working environment)	3	(0 – 3)	
Relevant contribution to management (rotas, committees etc)	3	(0 – 3)	
IT skills	2	(0 – 2)	

DESIRABLE CRITERIA

Assessed in Section	DESIRABLE CRITERIA	Max Score	Available Score	Applicant score
Part 2, A	Intercalated BSc, BA, MSc etc	1	0 or 1	
Part 2, A	Other relevant degrees or diplomas	2	(0 – 2)	
Part 2, A	MD or PhD (Note: only score if awarded for defending a thesis; *not* for primary or secondary medical degree. This usually equates to 2-3 years spent in pure research with minimal clinical activity)	3	0 or 3	
Part 2, A	Academic prizes and honours	2	(0 – 2)	
Part 2, D	Relevant experience in other specialties which would complement a career in O&G	1	(0 or 1)	
Part 2, E1				
Part 2, E1				
Part 2, E2	Extracurricular activities/achievements relevant to career in O&G	2	(0 – 2)	
Part 2, E2				

OTHER ACHIEVEMENTS & PERSONAL SKILLS – PART 2, SECTION G

Communication and interpersonal skills	3	(0 – 3)	Part 2, G
Problem-solving, decision-making & situational awareness	3	(0 – 3)	Part 2, G
Clearly demonstrates drive and initiative	3	(0 – 3)	Part 2, G

ACADEMIC ACHIEVEMENTS (Research, Presentations & Publications) & TEACHING – PART 2, SECTION H

Research experience (1 for a 1 year funded-post, 2 for appropriate MD, PhD experience, usually equating to 2-3 years in pure research with minimal clinical activity)	2	(0 – 2)	Part 2, H
Relevant peer-reviewed papers (1 per paper – **not** case reports, abstracts or letters)	3	(0 – 3)	Part 2, H
Other publications (1 per book chapter, book editor, case report – **not** abstracts or letters)	2	(0 – 2)	Part 2, H
Presentations (oral or poster) at international, national or regional meetings – **not** local meetings	2	(0 – 2)	Part 2, H
Teaching achievement (inc attendance at teaching courses etc)	2	(0 – 2)	Part 2, H

GENERAL ASSESSMENT – (Commitment to Specialty, Personal Development, etc) – PART 2, SECTIONS I, J & THE WHOLE APPLICATION FORM

Appropriate career progression consistent with personal circumstances and level of application	3	(0 – 3)	Part 2, I
Reasons for applying to this particular post	3	(0 – 3)	Part 2, I
Learning & Personal development	3	(0 – 3)	Part 2, J

ESSENTIAL CRITERIA - Sub total (ex 36)

DESIRABLE CRITERIA - Sub total (ex 22)

TOTAL SCORE (ex 58) =   (Transfer to table on next page)

© The Royal College of Obstetricians and Gynaecologists

	SCORE	COMMENT
A. TOTAL SCORE from previous page (ex 58)		This is the score used for FINAL RANKING
B. ACADEMIC SCORE - add up sections A and H (ex 19)		
Now subtract score (B) from score (A) giving:- SCORE FOR CLINICAL/ATTITUDINAL COMPONENTS (ex 39)		MUST SCORE A MINIMUM OF 21 TO BE CONSIDERED FOR SHORTLISTING

1. Maximum score (58) = Clinical/Attitudinal Score (39) + Academic Score [sections A and H] (19)
2. Minimum score to be considered for short-listing at ST1 level is 21 for clinical/attitudinal score
3. However, please note that if an applicant achieves this score, he/she will not automatically be short-listed. This is the minimum standard which must be achieved
4. The final shortlist for interview will reflect the ranking of applicants applying to the deanery (& will include the academic scores)
5. Any attributes which are evaluated on the basis of the application form alone may be further explored at the interview

SUITABLE FOR SHORTLISTING ST1 (minimum 21 for clinical/attitudinal):   YES / NO

ASSESSOR (print name): _____

DATE: _____

Chapter 8
Deanery Contacts

Obstetrics and Gynaecology 2010 Recruitment

Deanery Contacts

Deanery	Web Address	E-Mail
East Midlands	http://www.eastmidlandsdeanery.nhs.uk/	medicalrecruitment2010@eastmidlands.nhs.uk
East of England	http://www.eoedeanery.nhs.uk/	recruitment.helpdesk@eoe.nhs.uk
London/KSS (London)	http://www.londondeanery.ac.uk/	Obstetrics@londondeanery.ac.uk
London/KSS (KSS)	http://www.kssdeanery.org/	o&g@kssdeanery.ac.uk
Mersey	http://www.merseydeanery.nhs.uk/	2010recruitmentenquiries@merseydeanery.nhs.uk
North Western	http://www.nwpgmd.nhs.uk/	Helpdesk.Recruitment@pat.nhs.uk
Northern	http://www.northerndeaneryrecruitment.nhs.uk/	scott.hunter@nhs.net
Oxford	http://www.nesc.nhs.uk/	pgmde_recruitment@oxford-pgmde.co.uk
Severn	http://severndeanery.org.uk/	severn.stsupport@southwest.nhs.uk
South West Peninsula	http://www.peninsuladeanery.nhs.uk/	swphelpdesk@peninsuladeanery.ac.uk
Wales	http://www.cardiff.ac.uk/pgmde/	stjobs@cardiff.ac.uk
Wessex	http://www.nesc.nhs.uk/	wessexrecruitment@nesc.nhs.uk
West Midlands	http://www.westmidlandsdeanery.nhs.uk/	Use electronic helpdesk
Yorkshire & the Humber	http://www.yorksandhumberdeanery.nhs.uk/	specialtyrecruitment@yorksandhumber.nhs.uk

Chapter 9
Other Useful Resources

Useful list of website links

The Royal College of Obstetricians and Gynaecologists
http://www,rcog.org.uk/
https://obsjobs.rcog.org.uk/

British Medical Association
http://www.bma.org.uk/ap.nsf/content/home

British Medical Association's Doctors for Doctors Unit
Tel 08459 200 169 or info.d4d@bma.org.uk

Conference of Postgraduate Dental Deans & Directors
(COPDenD)
http://www.copdend.org.uk

Conference of Postgraduate Medical Education Deans of the
UK (COPMeD)
http://www.copmed.org.uk

Council of Heads of Medical Schools (CHMS)
http://www.chms.ac.uk/

Department of Health
http://www.dh.gov.uk/en/index.htm

e-learning for Healthcare
www.e-lfh.org.uk

Foundation Programme
http://www.foundationprogramme.nhs.uk/pages/home

Foundation Assessment Programme (Healthcare Assessment and Training)
http://www.hcat.nhs.uk

General Medical Council (GMC)
http://www.gmc-uk.org/

Joint Committee on Postgraduate Training for General Practice (JCPTGP)
http://www.jcptgp.org.uk/

MMC Inquiry led by Professor Sir John Tooke
http://www.mmcinquiry.org.uk/index.htm

MMC in Northern Ireland
http://www.nimdta.gov.uk/mmc

MMC in Scotland
http://www.mmc.scot.nhs.uk/

MMC in Wales
http://www.mmcwales.org/

Medical Research Council
http://www.mrc.ac.uk/index.htm

National Association of Clinical Tutors (NACT)
http://www.nact.org.uk/

National Association of Medical Personnel Specialists (NAMPS)
http://www.namps.org.uk/index.html

National Coordinating Centre for Research Capacity
http://www.nccrcd.nhs.uk/

NHS Careers
http://www.nhscareers.nhs.uk/

NHS Confederation
http://www.nhsconfed.org/

NHS Employers
http://www.nhsemployers.org/

NHS Institute for Innovation and Improvement
http://www.institute.nhs.uk/

NHS Jobs
http://www.jobs.nhs.uk/

National Medical Careers Fair
http://careersfair.bmj.com/

Postgraduate Medical Education and Training Board
http://www.pmetb.org.uk

ROSE (website for refugee doctors)
http://www.rose.nhs.uk/index.html

Skills for Health
http://www.skillsforhealth.org.uk/

For contact details of NHS Trusts in England & Wales please
see appendix on page 123.

Part 2
Chapter 1
General Advice

Homework

Congratulations on being shortlisted. By now you will have received notification of the date and time of your interview with the deanery. You may be in the position of having been shortlisted for two deaneries and having to prepare for two interviews, possibly with slightly different formats. Whatever your situation, you are likely to be feeling elated with the knowledge that you've cleared the first hurdle, but scared stiff by the prospect of facing the interview panel. These are normal reactions and feelings. The key point here, is to gain cognitive control and keep control. Unless you do so, you will spin off in a catastrophic wheel of self doubt and negative energy. Remember, because you've been shortlisted, you can be appointed, the job is yours to take. You've made the grade, keep that in your mind and build your preparation for the interview around this.

Preparation, preparation, preparation. To ensure you are offered a training post at interview, you must do your homework. At home make sure you know your curriculum vitae and application form inside out. If you've completed any audits, make sure you know what the auditable standards were, your methodology, results and any changes in practise that were implemented. Was the audit loop closed? If not, why not? What did you learn? What would you do differently next time? Put yourself in the interviewer's shoes, what would they want to know? The same is true of any publications. Practice the form of words you will use to convey, your expertise in these areas. You should be able to deliver concise and confident answers. Once you've decided on the form of words you would use, practise them out loud and then with colleagues, ideally with a senior one, either your Specialist Registrar, your Consultant or your educational supervisor.

2.1

As well as refreshing yourself with your achievements to date, you should also take time to research the deanery you are to be interviewed in. Try and find out the interview format, track down a successful applicant from the last round of appointments and glean any tips from them. Familiarise yourself with the hospitals within the deanery, where you may be rotated to. Elicit what subspecialty training is available within the deanery and find out what research opportunities there are. As a measure of the research and publication output of the deanery, Google or check Pub Med for the names of Consultants within the Hospitals and University Medical School. The more active they are, the more they will have published. A list of research grants is also important. The more successful grant applications, the more successful the department. Another indicator is the number of higher degrees, such as MD or PhD that have been awarded. Good supervisors, will have a good track record of research fellows who have been successful in attaining a higher degree.

What about teaching and educational supervision within the deanery? Some deaneries have well established programmes, with a day release a month, which are well attended and well received by trainees. Others have not. Some may have a well developed IT system with online resources for trainees. Others may not. Find out what the strengths and weaknesses are for the deanery you are going to be interviewed in, so that you can allude to them in your interview and thus demonstrate that you have done your homework. It is all about demonstrating your knowledge, in a competitive way, to place you ahead of your fellow interviewees.

The night before the interview
It might seem obvious but if you have far to travel, travel the night before. Deaneries will pay reasonable interview expenses, including travel, subsistence and overnight stay. Don't try and drive in rush hour traffic over long distances, the morning of your interview. You will only end up late and feeling even more

stressed. The interview panel will also take a dim view of you being late. If you can't even make it on time to your interview, what chance have you got of being punctual at handovers on the labour ward and reliably turning up to clinic, ward rounds etc? Don't drink more than one or two units of alcohol and go to bed early. Exercise in the early evening may be of benefit but don't play that league game of squash at 9 o'clock as you will only end up lying in bed awake until 1 o'clock, in the morning and reduce your chances of delivering your best performance the following day.

Child care can often be difficult, especially if you are breast feeding a baby. Plan in advance, express and refrigerate or freeze. You can refrigerate breast milk for 3 -5 days and freeze it for 3 months. Put yourself first. Your partner, mother, child minder or friend will be able to cope without you. It's really important you are as refreshed as possible.

You might want to read through your notes one last time, but no more than this. If you want to read something medical, browse the BMJ or the editorial of the BJOG.

The day of the interview
When it comes to what to wear, it's all about projecting the right image. You want to appear professional; how you dress, like it or not, is very important. Unfortunately it's subjective and what is acceptable for one interviewer may not be acceptable for another. As a general rule the medical profession is conservative and whilst the dress code in hospital has become more relaxed and informal in recent years, this is not the case at interview. For women you should have your hair up, avoid high heels and plunging neck lines. When it comes to jewellery keep it simple, a broach, a necklace, something to highlight a feature, but not to cause a distraction. For men a dark suit and tie is still the preferred uniform. If you've bought an "interview suit" make sure you take off the shop label (especially on the cuff) . If

you've bought a new shirt, make sure you iron it and that it's the right collar size. It should fit snugly round your neck. If you suffer with dandruff make sure you shampoo with Nizoral® (or equivalent) every three to four days for two to four weeks before your interview.

Before you are called in, spend some time warming up your voice and muscles of the facial mask. This is really important as it helps power your voice, reduces the likelihood of mumbling and gives your voice a richness in tone. For exercises to practise look at OSCEs for the MRCOG Vol 1 & 2 available from our website at www.daltonsquaremedical.co.uk.

When you are called in, remember to smile, make eye contact with everyone on the panel and if possible or if you are given the opportunity, shake their hands. Touch is a very good way of connecting with a person and the start of building up a rapport with them. Avoid introducing yourself by a nickname, "Hi I'm Johnny". This may be okay for speed dating but it is too informal in this setting, use your full name.

Finally be conscious of your body language. If you get the opportunity to observe yourself on film, perhaps in the context of a consultation, take it and critically appraise your body language. Use your hands to emphasise a particular point or to add movement to refocus the interviewer on yourself, if they appear not to be concentrating, but avoid "David Bellamy" hands. For those of you not familiar with this reference, it's the use of wild and extreme hand movements. Waving them in the air like a baboon. Avoid crossing your knees and keep your hands folded in front of you, don't start fidgeting. It is surprising how many of us have tics that emerge when we are under pressure. Avoid saying 'mmmm' at the start of every answer, nodding all the time and rocking your chair. I know it is a lot to remember. That is why it is important to practise. In many respects, you are giving a performance. The more you rehearse

the better the performance (interview) you will give.
The next two chapters accompany the online videos. View them critically. Use them as a basis from which to develop and produce your own interview performance.

Remember the job is yours to take. If you are unsuccessful on this occasion view it as deferred success. Reflect on the things you did well and the things you would do differently next time. "Break a leg" as actors say.

2.1

Chapter 2

Accessing the online videos

Your purchase of this book entitles you to view our free online videos especially produced to support this text.

Using Flash streaming technology you can now view filmed interviews demonstrating how you should and should not respond when interviewed, some vital tips and much more.

ACTIVATE YOUR FREE ONLINE ACCESS

STEP 1
Visit: www.daltonsquaremedical.co.uk/obsfree

STEP 2
Follow the instructions to access the sign up form to request your login details.

STEP 3
Once we have confirmed your details we will email you to let you know you can login to the Video resource.

And that's it.

Once your Login details have been confirmed you can access the Video resource whenever you wish and view the video content directly in your browser.
Should you have any difficulty accessing the sign-up section or registering online please feel free to contact us at:

enquiries@daltonsquaremedical.co.uk

or on   +44 (0)1202 707738

2.2

Our contact details, along with links to our other acclaimed medical teaching resources can also be found on our main site at: www.daltonsquaremedical.co.uk

Chapter 3

Portfolio Station

A.Umranikar, Specialist Registrar
K.Madhvani, Specialist Registrar
J. Mountfield, Director of Education Southampton University

Key points on portfolio: at this station the examiner will interview you on your portfolio/CV.

Remember a few starting tips:
Your CV is your ticket to progress in the job race. As your CV has been shortlisted, it has passed the initial test. It is the only part of the job interview process where you as a candidate should have 100% control. i.e. know your CV well. Your CV is used to provide a structure to the job interview and will often prompt your first question to put you at ease.

At this station, the examiner is looking for 4 areas that reflect you as a good candidate namely:

Your knowledge, skills, experience and attitude.

This is an example of a practice interview for ST1/2. For ST3 interview, the structure remains the same although your work experience will be more than an ST1 candidate.

2.3

i - Question 1
"Talk me through your CV"

Interviewer seated, candidate walks into shot and says good morning

Interviewer: "Good morning. Please have a seat."

Candidate sits down.

Interviewer: "Talk me through your CV please."

Candidate: "My name is Linda Snell, and I am currently a Foundation Year 2 doctor in Southampton General Hospital.
I graduated from Southampton Medical School in 2008 and did my Foundation year 1 in Basingstoke. I rotated through acute medicine, care of the elderly and upper GI surgery. I then came back to Southampton for my Foundation year 2 and started off in Accident & Emergency for 4 months before rotating into Obstetrics and Gynaecology."

Interviewer: "Ok, quite an assortment of specialities then. What have you learnt that will be helpful in a career of Obstetrics and Gynaecology?"

Candidate: "All of my jobs have given me the opportunity to develop my skills and confidence in history taking and basic procedures such as cannulation, arterial blood gas sampling and urethral catheterisation.

In medicine I worked within small teams, especially in the care of the elderly, where I learnt the importance of communicating effectively with

2.3
i

not only medical colleagues, but also with other healthcare professionals.

My surgical attachment gave me the opportunity to go to theatre and to learn how to care for post-operative patients, about the monitoring involved and gave me insight into potential complications. I also became familiar with modified early warning charts and their clinical relevance."

Interviewer: "How have you used these skills practically?"

Candidate: "I utilised, all these skills during my Accident and Emergency attachment. Here I also learnt how to independently assess and commence basic life support on the acutely unwell patient, as well as presenting concise histories to my seniors when I needed help. It also taught me to remain calm and organised under pressure which has been really useful when I've been on call."

Interviewer: "That's good Linda, and how are you enjoying Obstetrics and Gynaecology?"

Candidate: "I am really enjoying being in such a dynamic environment where every day is different!

I enjoy Obstetrics, it's so unique, in that the women are generally young and healthy and we help to manage a physiological process where the outcomes are nearly always positive!

Gynaecology is so varied; I enjoy assessing acute admissions and developing my examination skills as well as taking focused histories in clinic. I also enjoy going to theatre and I am planning on doing the basic practical skills course as soon as possible.

I like the unique combination of medicine and surgery and the variety of the workload."

Key points: (Voiceover)

The examiner is looking for:

Brief chronology of your training (20seconds)

Description of relevant experience and skills attained so far from the training posts (2-4/points) which would be developed in the speciality.

Finally you may choose to summarise yourself as:
Competent, dynamic, hard working, professional, thorough and reliable. (or pick your top 3 qualities)

2.3 i

Common mistakes:

Do not literally take them though your CV

Do not go through every single job – answer should be structured around the main themes of your experience. You simply need to convert your training experience into something that is easy to listen to.

Be concise- this is usually a warm up question.

Marking scheme:

0- Information listed but without examples
1- Good structure but limited information provided
2- Information is accurate providing concrete examples of achievements

	0	1	2
Score:	☐	☐	☐

ii - Question 2
"Why Obstetrics & Gynaecology?"

Interviewer: "Why do you want to train in Obstetrics & Gynaecology?

Candidate: "I really enjoyed my time in Obstetrics & Gynaecology as a medical student.

I've always thought Obstetrics & Gynaecology to be a good mix of medicine and surgery. I believe the speciality offers a wide range of clinical exposure from ward work, to clinics and to theatres. I also enjoy the challenge of dealing with patients in difficult and often sensitive situations and being part of a team with a skill set able to make a real difference to women and their partners."

Interviewer: "Can you expand a little on the wide range of clinical exposure?"

Candidate: "Yes. The variety within the speciality, is what I've always enjoyed.

You can experience days full of joy delivering babies while on the other hand you also have the opportunity to help patients through difficult times – for example dealing with women with miscarriages, ectopic pregnancies or cancers.

I've also enjoyed the buzz of working on labour ward with the challenge of working in a multidisciplinary team.

I can appreciate the importance of effective

2.3
ii

communication to ensure safety of our patients and also to reduce the possible conflicts that can develop as a result of shared responsibilities."

Interviewer: "What about Gynaecology?"

Candidate: "It's so varied; I enjoy assessing acute admissions and the challenge of successful resuscitation of the young women attending with acute gynaecological emergencies. I also enjoy the surgical exposure and am planning to do the basic practical skills course as soon as possible."

Interviewer: "and what about on a personal level?"

Candidate: "From a personal perspective, I feel the holistic approach that this field offers is very rewarding. I've attended contraception and sexual health clinics alongside general gynaecology clinics and appreciate how much professional help and advice we can offer to women of all ages, from their adolescent to their post menopausal years."

Key points: (Voiceover)

Your answer should be structured around 3 or 4 clear reasons:

Speciality specific reasons: The variety of work load the speciality offers, or good mix of medicine and surgery. This may be a cliché but is the reason most people choose the speciality.
A holistic approach needed in dealing with sensitive issues related to pregnancy.
Good mix of independent work and teamwork.
Strong multidisciplinary influence.

Personal reasons: The challenge of dealing with difficult patients and sensitive situations.

Academic reasons: A rapidly advancing speciality, or good opportunities for teaching and research.
Enjoy the teaching aspect of learning through simulation techniques used in obstetric drills.

Common mistakes:

I want to train in this field because I think it is an interesting and challenging speciality and I feel that I have a lot to contribute to this field.
There is no real attempt of reasoning with examples or personal stories to back the answer. (This is an opportunity to demonstrate how suitable you are to train in obstetrics and gynaecology).

Marking scheme:

2.3
ii

    0-   vague answer with no structure or examples
    1-   some evidence provided but relevance to the speciality not explained
    2-   one good example provided with correct relevance to the speciality
    3-   More than 1 example provided with good reasoning.

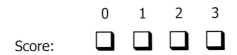

iii - Question 3
"Why this Deanery?"

Interviewer: "Why do you want to train in this deanery?"

Candidate: "I've applied for a post in this deanery for a number of reasons.
This deanery offers a huge variety of hospital settings. There is a good selection of large, very busy and specialised centres and smaller district general hospitals."

Interviewer: "True, but isn't that the case for the other deaneries?"

Candidate: "Yes, but the deanery also covers a varied population, providing a good case mix for training.

One of the biggest assets of the deanery is that it actively encourages an involvement in research. I have already been involved in a few research projects as a medical student and wish to participate in other research activities.

I also have an interest in teaching and would like to take advantage of the opportunities to get involved in the undergraduate teaching programme.

Finally, I have talked to a number of trainees and also looked at the PMETB data which suggests that this deanery offers an excellent standard of training."

2.3
iii

Common mistakes: (Voice over)

Say you have looked at the PMETB data when you haven't!

I wish to train in or around London because of the variety of population and the different experiences that I can gain in that region.

This answer is not effective as the candidate has made no effort to research the training scheme and to describe what aspects of the training scheme are of particular benefit to him/her.

It is acceptable to give social reasons if you have them, but only after you have successfully demonstrated the knowledge of the training programme of the deanery.

Marking scheme:

0- No clear reasoning with examples
1- Vague geographical or social reasons not relating to the training programme
2- Limited understanding of the training programme
3- Reasonable to good understanding of the training programme with clear reasons
4- Excellent understanding of the training programme with clear and detailed explanations of the reasons

iv - Question 4
"What Personal Attributes do you have?"

Interviewer: "What skills or personal attributes do you possess that will make you a good trainee in this speciality?"

Candidate: "I am able to stay calm under pressure and at the same time I can take the initiative in challenging situations."

Interviewer: "Can you give me a recent example?"

Candidate: "Yes. I was recently faced with an agitated patient who was pregnant in labour with a history of substance abuse. I could see the patient becoming more agitated and I was concerned about her becoming violent. I was able to communicate effectively with the patient and was also able to calm her down with the help of a midwife. It took a while, but by involving and asking my senior colleagues for help, I worked as an effective member of a multidisciplinary team involving midwives, obstetricians, anaesthetists and neonatologists all of which contributed to a good outcome for the patient."

Interviewer: "Excellent, have you any other attributes?"

Candidate: "I believe I am a good listener, able to engage with patients and that I have the ability to empathise and be sensitive in difficult situations."

Interviewer: "Good can you give me an example of such a situation?"

2.3
iv

Candidate: "I recently had to break bad news to a patient that she had suffered a miscarriage after receiving fertility treatment. I was able to communicate effectively with the patient and with the help of the nurses in the Early Pregnancy Assessment Unit, we managed to support the woman and her partner through a very emotional and devastating experience. As well as managing the initial emotionally labile situation I offered follow up counselling to help the patient and her partner get closure."

Key points:

This is a broad question which may leave you puzzled because you do not know from where to start the answer.

Your answer should reflect a good understanding of the speciality and the skills and the attributes which you will need.

You should be able to demonstrate using examples that you possess those skills and attributes.

To succeed in obstetrics and gynaecology, you need to be able to cope with pressured situations, work well in a team and communicate effectively.

You also need to have good practical skills.

Maintain clarity in your answer which will come from the structure backed by concise examples.

Marking scheme:

0- Vague reasons

1- Skills and attributes explained but little relevance to the speciality and without examples

2- Good clarity and structure with an ability to demonstrate making full use of personal experiences relevant to the speciality

	0	1	2
Score:	☐	☐	☐

v - Question 5
"What Courses have you done?"

Interviewer: "I can see you've done some courses, tell me about them."

Candidate: "Yes, during my Foundation Year 1 I initially did a Acute Life Threatening Events, Recognition and Treatment course to help me develop a framework to assess acutely unwell patients.

As the year progressed I developed these skills and gained more experience. I then did the Advanced Life Support course to build on this foundation and to help me prepare for my A&E job. I found it really useful as I am now confident in the acute situation and can initiate treatment independently."

Interviewer: "I see you've been on the Basic Practical Skills Course, what did you learn from this."

Candidate: "It gave me the opportunity to really focus on my basic technique, so that I can maximise the learning opportunities during my Obstetrics and Gynaecology attachment. The course taught me basic knot tying and sub-cuticular suturing.

I have also attended "skills and drills" sessions in this attachment and my next objective is to do the Advanced Life Support in Obstetrics course."

Interviewer: "Very good, thank you."

2.3
v

vi - Question 6
"What Teaching have you done?"

Interviewer: "I see you have had some experience in teaching. Tell me about this please."

Candidate: "I've always enjoyed teaching and I find I learn a lot from it. In preparing for a teaching session, I have to ensure, that I've got the requisite factual knowledge, this means that I have to make the time to read the topic in depth.

I've taught different groups of students at undergraduate and postgraduate level and utilised a variety of teaching methods."

Interviewer: "Tell me a little bit about your undergraduate teaching?"

Candidate: "I've done regular tutorials for 3rd year students where I had to prepare the tutorial topic.

I've also been a tutor for 2nd year students. In this role I took small group seminars, typically of 5 students. I also got involved in the demonstration of basic practical clinical skills."

Interviewer: "Have you been on any teaching courses?"

Candidate: "Yes, I've attended the "tomorrow's teaching" course aimed at Clinicians who want to develop good teaching skills.

I've also been involved in workshops for the Advanced Life Support course.

I've had very positive feedback from students and introduced improvements, based on constructive criticism. In the future I plan to get a degree in medical education and to continue in a teaching role, in parallel with my clinical commitments."

Interviewer: "Thank you."

Key points: (Voiceover)

This is a fairly straightforward question.

Your answer should go beyond the day-to-day informal teaching experiences that you may have had.

Don't say you are interested in education unless you really are!

Marking scheme:

0- No structure regarding the teaching experience
1- Informal teaching experience only
2- Organised teaching sessions in form of workshops, departmental presentations or teaching undergraduates
3- Good structure and initiative demonstrated in organising different types teaching sessions or targets groups and demonstrating the effort to prepare own lectures.

	0	1	2	3
Score:	☐	☐	☐	☐

vii - Question 7
"What Audit have you done?"

Interviewer: "I see you 've done a couple of audits, can you tell me about your most recent audit, please."

Candidate: "I've carried out three audits in the past two years. Two of these resulted in improvements to patient care and I led them personally from initiation to conclusion.

The most recent audit I did was during my Accident and Emergency placement. I was the lead auditor and I looked at the use of plain abdominal x-rays."

Interviewer: "and why did you chose this area to audit?"

Candidate: "Well within the first few weeks of the job, I noticed that we seemed to do a lot of x-rays which didn't seem to change many management plans. I was concerned about the level of radiation patients were exposed to and about the financial cost to the department.

I used guidelines issued by the Royal College of Radiologists to set the audit standards. I then looked through the notes to see if the requesting doctor had documented their interpretation of the film, and matched it up with the formal radiology report.

The results showed that over 70% of the films were inappropriately requested; only 30% had a documented interpretation of the film in the notes and less than 5% of films showed positive pathology."

Interviewer: "So what did you do with these results?"

Candidate: "Following the audit we introduced a set of guidelines. All requests must now be verified by the A&E registrars. In addition, all the A&E doctors, must have formal teaching from the Radiologists to help improve their interpretation of films. I presented the audit at our audit meeting and it was well received."

Interviewer: "And have these changes improved patient safety or delivered any cost improvements?"

Candidate: "Once the changes have been in place for 6 months I plan to repeat the audit, to "close the audit loop" . Based on the experience of my earlier audits, I would expect to see a reduction of inappropriate requests and a reduction in the recharges from Radiology to the Accident & Emergency department."

Interviewer: "Thank you."

Key points: (Voiceover)

The interviewer will assess you on the following criteria:

Number of audits.

Most junior doctors are expected to complete one audit per post or 2 per year.

Your role in the audit.

Usefulness of your audit

Understanding the audit cycle

Presentation of audit results

Marking scheme:

0- No audits conducted

1- Explanation of the audit results but unclear regarding understanding of the audit process and the description of the audit cycle

2- Good understanding of the audit process with clear description of the audit results. A good understanding of the audit cycle.

	0	1	2
Score:	☐	☐	☐

2.3
vii

"Tell me about a mistake you made"

Interviewer: "Tell me about a time you made a mistake. What did you learn?"

Candidate: "In my foundation year 2, I was asked to review the results of an antenatal patient whose haemoglobin was 8.0g/dl. I acted on the result and advised oral iron for the patient. The advice was communicated to the GP."

Interviewer: "Sounds reasonable?"

Candidate: "Yes but two weeks later the patient presented in established labour. She had not taken the prescription and her haemoglobin was still 8. I was the junior doctor on call. I made sure that the patient was grouped and saved and had 4 units of blood cross matched. I also secured intravenous access."

Interviewer: "Go on."

Candidate: "Post partum her haemoglobin dropped to 6 and with her consent she underwent a four unit transfusion."

Interviewer: "Was the case investigated?"

Candidate: "Yes, the case was discussed at the clinical risk meeting. It was felt that if this patient had been seen sooner antenatally, there would have been an opportunity to correct her anaemia using intravenous iron prior to delivery which would have prevented blood transfusion. The patient

2.3
viii

was also found to be a late booker in pregnancy and had not attended several antenatal visits."

(Result/Reflection):

Interviewer: "OK, you've shared with me a clinical incident, but what did you learn from this?"

Candidate: "Well I first reflected and discussed the case with my consultant.

I realised that it was clearly a mistake to action a result without knowing clinical details of the patient particularly in pregnancy where a low haemoglobin result could have been corrected prior to delivery."

Interviewer: "and anything else?"

Candidate: "I also missed the opportunity to recall the patient to the clinic given her history of poor antenatal attendance.

The labour ward team, also forgot to put an incident form which was a learning point in its own right.

I was however praised for being a good team member, for arranging blood efficiently when this lady was labouring and ensuring prompt blood transfusion thus preventing further morbidity."

Examiner: "Thank you."

Candidate: "Thank you."

Key points: (Voiceover)

This question tests your ability to recognise mistakes, take responsibility for your mistakes, sort them out, reflect on your experience and modify your clinical practice accordingly.
The interviewers are trying to establish that you are safe in clinical practice, and as far as you are concerned, when mistakes happen, you can deal with them appropriately.
You can mention any mistake- a clinical or a non clinical one unless the interviewers have directed you to a particular one.

Common mistake:

Do not describe a mistake of another colleague.
The interviewer wants you to demonstrate your honesty and integrity as a clinician.
Everyone on the panel has been a junior doctor sometime and therefore knows what it's like in the early days!
There's no point pretending to be perfect in such situations.

2.3
viii

Marking scheme:

  0   No mistakes made
  1.   Describes the mistake but does not reflect on own future practice.
  2.   Clearly demonstrates ability to recognise mistakes, reflects on own experience and modifies clinical practice accordingly

                    0   1   2
Score: ☐ ☐ ☐

TOTAL SCORE: ☐

References:

1. Max Eggert. Perfect CV:2003 edition

2. Olivier Picard, Dan Wood, Sebastian Yuen- Medical interviews. A Comprehensive Guide to CT,ST & Registrar Interview Skills

3. Mo Shapiro, Alison Straw. Tackling Interview Questions in a week.2002

4. R. Chambers: Career planning for everyone in the NHS. The Toolkit

Chapter 4
Clinical Station OSCE

The Management of Post Operative Hypotension
By Alec McEwan, RCOG College Tutor.

i - "Good Candidate" (Candidate A)

You are the SHO on-call. It is 7pm and you are called to the gynaecology ward to see a post-operative patient that the nursing staff have concerns about. Mrs B is a 54 year old woman who underwent total abdominal hysterectomy and bilateral salpingo-oophorectomy earlier in the day. Her pulse is a regular 112 beats per minute and her BP is 80/50.

Explain to the interviewer how you would initially approach this problem. You can ask for further information if you wish.

Dialogue

Interviewer: "Good morning. Do you understand what we are asking you to do at this station? Imagine that you are the on call senior house officer. It is 7pm and you have been called to the gynaecology ward by the nursing staff. Mrs B is a 54 year old woman who underwent total abdominal hysterectomy and bilateral salpingo-oophorectomy earlier in the day. Her pulse is a regular 112 beats per minute and her BP is 80/50. This is not a role playing scenario. All I need you to do is to explain to me what you would do if you were faced by this clinical problem."

Candidate: "I would begin by introducing myself to Mrs B, and explaining who I am and why I have been asked to see her. I would ask her if she was in any pain? I would then proceed to make an initial

2.4
i

101

assessment of Mrs B, following the common steps in resuscitation. A, B, C....... Airway, breathing, circulation....... Am I correct to assume she doesn't have an airway problem, and that she is breathing regularly? What is her respiratory rate?"

Interviewer: "Yes, she has no airway compromise, and is able to communicate with you. Her pain is under control and she has a respiratory rate of 20 breaths per minute."

Candidate: "Hmm, that is quite elevated. I would start some facial oxygen, and raise the foot end of the bed if possible. I would lay her flat. Focussing on 'C', her circulation, I would feel the volume of her pulse, its rate and regularity. Does she have intravenous access? What intravenous fluids is she receiving? Can I ask if she is catheterised? What is her urine output?

Interviewer: "Yes, she is catheterised. She has produced a total of 100 mls of clear urine since the operation. Her pulse is now 120 and regular, but feels thready. She has a green cannula in situ, which is running a litre bag of normal saline slowly over 8 hours."

Candidate: "My principal concern is that Mrs B has on-going haemorrhage. She needs good IV access, and that means siting at least one large bore cannula. A second one may be necessary if the green one is not working well. Whilst siting this cannula I would take blood for a four unit urgent blood cross-match, full blood count, clotting studies and electrolytes. I would ask the nursing staff to organise labelling and sending off these bloods urgently. I would ask one of them to alert my registrar on-call. Whilst doing this, I would also ask what time the operation was performed and how much IV fluid has been given since theatre. Did Mrs B lose much blood intra-operatively? I am also keen to know if Mrs B has any underlying medical problems. I would ask Mrs B myself, but I would also been keen to review the notes personally. Does she have any family history that might be relevant?"

Interviewer: "One of the nurses goes to collect and review the notes, whilst another starts labelling the blood samples. What else might you do at this point?

Candidate: "I need to examine Mrs B but she also needs urgent volume expansion. It is a priority that the cross-match is requested urgently but whilst the blood is awaited I would ask that a unit of colloid, such as Gelofusin, be given immediately through the wide bore cannula. I would follow this with intravenous crystalloid"

Interviewer: "Which crystalloid would you choose? Are there any fluids that you wouldn't use? How fast would you give the intravenous fluid?"

Candidate: "I would use Hartmann's or Normal saline. I would avoid 5% dextrose because it stays in the intravascular space less time than the others. The fluid needs to be given quickly, but care would need to be exercised if Mrs B had other health problems, particularly cardiac."

Interviewer: "What would you be looking for on examination?"

2.4
i

Candidate: "I would want to know if there been significant vaginal bleeding. Are there any drains? If there are, how much blood is in them? Is her abdomen distended? Is the abdomen resonant to percussion? Can I hear bowel sounds? I would like to see the wound. Is there a haematoma forming? Are her heart and lungs clear?

Interviewer: "Her abdomen is somewhat distended and dull to percussion. There is minimal loss on her pad, and no drains were sited during the operation. There is a slight ooze from the wound, but nothing remarkable. Apart from the tachycardia, hypotension and raised respiratory rate, cardio respiratory examination is unremarkable. The lungs are clear and the heart sounds are normal. You note she has a raised body mass index.

One of the nurses returns with the notes. On review, you see that Mrs B is an insulin dependent diabetic, and that she is normally treated for hypertension. Her body mass index is 38. A first degree relative suffered with a DVT following a road traffic accident. Mrs B has had a hysterectomy today because of endometrial hyperplasia with atypical change. Intra-operative blood loss was 350 mls and she has had one litre of fluid in total since the start of the operation. The surgery was apparently straightforward."

Candidate: "What medications is she on normally?

Interviewer: "She takes daily low dose aspirin, an ACE inhibitor, and a statin. She normally self-administers Novomix twice a day but she is currently on a sliding scale.

Candidate: "What is her most recent blood glucose level?"

Interviewer: "Her most recent BM, taken 20 minutes ago, was 5.6 mmol/L.

Candidate: "What analgesia has she received since theatre?"

Interviewer: "She has a morphine PCA. Also, she received one dose of low molecular weight heparin in recovery"

               Pause

               What thoughts are you having about the possible causes? What is your working diagnosis?"

Candidate: "I am concerned she has on-going bleeding. Everything is consistent with that, and the timing is right. However, other possibilities that I would be considering include.......... Well, she could simply be behind on fluid replacement. Also she has risk factors for either a cardiac event, or pulmonary embolus. Other symptoms and signs might be expected, but not necessarily so. Infection can cause tachycardia and hypotension, but would be unlikely so soon after the operation. Pain may contribute to a tachycardia, but Mrs B is not in pain. Opiates may contribute to hypotension, but this alone would not explain the full clinical picture."

Interviewer: "How would you confirm your suspicions, and exclude any other possibilities?"

Candidate: "I would consider performing an ECG and Chest

2.4
i

X-ray. Arterial blood gases might be valuable if I really thought a PE was likely, and cardiac enzymes if a cardiac event seems a possibility. I am particularly interested in the haemoglobin result though. That is the key. Is it ready yet?"

Interviewer: "Not quite yet. So far, you have been with Mrs B for fifteen minutes. Is there anything you would do whilst awaiting the haemoglobin level?"

Candidate: "I would explain to Mrs B my concerns, and set out my plan to her. If the registrar had not yet arrived I would take this opportunity to contact him or her myself to appraise him of the situation. I would ask the nurses for another set of observations"

Interviewer: "Your registrar is busy on labour ward and doesn't answer his bleep. The haemoglobin value comes back as 5.1 g/dl. The APTT is marginally raised. The nurse tells you that Mrs B now has a pulse of 124 per minute and that her BP is 70/45, despite the fluids."

Candidate: "I would be interested to know what her pre-operative haemoglobin value was, but the evidence is pointing strongly to primary haemorrhage. We need to commence a transfusion. How long will the blood take to come?"

Interviewer: "A nurse phones blood bank. They are predicting another 25 minutes still."

Candidate: "I would call the on-call consultant gynaecologist and state clearly that I believe Mrs B is suffering on-going bleeding and needs return to theatre immediately. I would expect him/her to come in, in view of the potential severity of the situation and the unavailability of the registrar. Provided the consultant agreed with me, I would then contact the on-call anaesthetist, and theatres, and explain that I have a case that needs theatre immediately. I would consider mobilising the O negative blood and I would liaise with the on-call haematologist and explain the likely need for more blood, and other blood products in view of the coagulopathy. I would do my best to keep a contemporaneous note of all these actions"

Interviewer: "Good. What would you say to Mrs B?"

Candidate: "I would take consent for examination under anaesthesia and laparotomy, explaining that we are likely to find on-going bleeding from one of the vessels in the pelvis. I would explain our strong recommendation that blood and blood products will be needed and ensure that she was OK with this. She might need further colloid, and some O Neg blood whilst the cross-matched blood arrives. I would stay with her on the journey back to theatre, unless the anaesthetist came to the ward. I would ask her if she wanted any relatives informing of events."

Interviewer: "Mrs B is found to have over 1.5 litres of blood in her abdomen at laparotomy. The bleeding has come from one of the pedicles and it takes some time for the consultant to get it under control. In total, Mrs B requires 8 units of blood, fresh frozen plasma and platelets. The anaesthetist decides that an overnight stay in ITU is safest. What

2.4
i

complications might Mrs B at risk of now?"

Candidate: "She is at risk of further haemorrhage, and intra-abdominal infection. The hypovolaemia, probable acidosis and massive blood transfusion put her at risk of hypothermia, metabolic disruption and pulmonary oedema or even adult respiratory distress syndrome. Any underlying coronary artery disease caused by her chronic hypertension and diabetes might be uncovered and present as a secondary cardiac event. Her risk of deep venous thrombosis and pulmonary embolism is now higher than it was previously. Her pre-operative hypotension might cause pre-renal failure, or even acute tubular necrosis. A second intubation and need for longer ventilation may increase the risks of chest infection. Her obesity and diabetes puts her at risk of wound infection. A prolonged ileus can follow intra-abdominal haemorrhage. She could still bleed again. I suspect the consultant would site a drain to help assess this risk"

Pauses, and looks thoughtful

"Recollection of the initial post-operative events might cause her serious anxiety at a later date. After all, she could have died."

Interviewer: "Mrs B actually is a patient on one of the other gynaecology firms to the one you normally work on. Does your involvement end there?"

Candidate: "On her return to the gynae ward I would take the opportunity to sit with Mrs B and ask if she has any questions. Unless the consultant had done so already, I would want to review the events of that evening with her if she wished. A risk management form should have been completed already, however I could do this if it had not.

Interviewer: "How do you learn from near-miss cases like this?

Candidate: "She would probably prove to be a valuable basis for formal reflective practice, or a case-based discussion. I would actively seek out feedback from the nursing and consultant staff regarding my own performance."

Interviewer: "Thankyou. You can move onto the next station"

2.4
i

Clinical Station OSCE

The Management of Post Operative Hypotension

ii - "Poor Candidate" (Candidate B)

You are the SHO on-call. It is 7pm and you are called to the gynaecology ward to see a post-operative patient that the nursing staff have concerns about. Mrs B is a 54 year old woman who underwent total abdominal hysterectomy and bilateral salpingo-oophorectomy earlier in the day. Her pulse is a regular 112 beats per minute and her BP is 80/50.

Explain to the interviewer how you would initially approach this problem. You can ask for further information if you wish.

Dialogue

Interviewer: "Good morning. Do you understand what we are asking you to do at this station? Imagine that you are the on call senior house officer. It is 7pm and you have been called to the gynaecology ward by the nursing staff. Mrs B is a 54 year old woman who underwent total abdominal hysterectomy and bilateral salpingo-oophorectomy earlier in the day. Her pulse is a regular 112 beats per minute and her BP is 80/50. This is not a role playing scenario. All I need you to do is to explain to me what you would do if you were faced by this clinical problem."

Candidate: "Hmmm. Well her BP seems a bit low, and her pulse is a bit fast. I would see if she is in pain and I would want to resuscitate her with intravenous fluids. She may still be dry from the operation."

Interviewer:	"She has a morphine PCA and is not in undue discomfort."
Candidate:	"The morphine may be causing her hypotension"
Interviewer:	"Possibly. Which fluids would you choose, and how fast would you give them?"
Candidate:	"Well, normal saline or dextrose"
Interviewer:	"Which would you prefer to use, and why?"
Candidate:	"I usually pick Normal saline; to replace the salts"
Interviewer:	"How fast would you give the IV fluids?"
Candidate:	"You could run the bag through 'stat'"
Interviewer:	"What 'bag' is that?"
Candidate:	"Well, a litre bag, I suppose"
Interviewer:	"Which type of fluid is better at supporting the blood pressure than crystalloid?"
Candidate:	"Oh. I suppose you could use some Gelo"
Interviewer:	Looking puzzled "Gelo?"
Candidate:	"Yes. Gelofusin" (Candidate looks a little confused, and completely fails to recognise that the interviewer is not impressed by the use of such abbreviations)

Interviewer: "Would you do anything else?"

Candidate: "I would check her urine output"

Interviewer: "It is 100mls since theatre, 6 hours ago"

Candidate: "Hmmm, she does seem dry. She needs that fluid"

Interviewer: "How are you communicating these instructions to the nursing staff?"

Candidate: Look of realisation on the face of the candidate "Oh yes, I see what you mean. I would be on the ward, with the patient, and I would ask the nurse directly"

Interviewer: "Good. The fluids are running, although rather slowly through the green cannula. Is there anything else you would do?"

Candidate: *Prolonged pause.*
"Check some bloods?"

Interviewer: "Any in particular? Why are you doing them?"

Candidate: "Full blood count, U & Es. ....well to check her electrolytes and her haemoglobin. The penny finally drops and the candidate realises what the interviewer is getting at. Oh, to see if she is bleeding!"

Interviewer: "Correct. What other evidence might you find to support this possibility?"

Candidate: "Erm. She may have vaginal bleeding"

2.4
ii

Interviewer:	"True. What other examination findings would you look for?"
Candidate:	"Perhaps pale conjunctivae. Also a low BP and a fast pulse. Low urine output....."
Interviewer:	Pauses to give the candidate time. "And her abdomen"
Candidate:	"Oh Oh yes. She may have a distended abdomen"
Interviewer:	"Her abdomen is somewhat distended and dull to percussion. There is minimal loss on her pad, and no drains were sited during the operation. There is a slight ooze from the wound, but nothing remarkable. Would you examine anything else?
Candidate:	"Yes, her heart and lungs"
Interviewer:	"Apart from the tachycardia and hypotension, she has a raised respiratory rate but otherwise cardio respiratory examination is unremarkable. Her lungs are clear, and she has normal heart sounds. You note she has a raised body mass index. What other possible explanations might there be for her condition? Are they likely?"
Candidate:	"Well, it seems pretty obvious that she is bleeding still. I have already mentioned that she might be in pain, or that the pain killers may be causing a low blood pressure........."
Interviewer:	Pauses to give the candidate time.
	"What else can cause hypotension?"

Candidate: "Ermmm......Infection?"

Interviewer: "Yes it can, but is that likely?"

Candidate: "Probably not. She has only just had her operation"

Interviewer: Pauses to give the candidate time. "You mentioned the opiates. Can any other drugs cause hypotension?"

Candidate: (Enthusiastically) Yes, anti-hypertensives can.

Interviewer: "So......." (examiner gesticulates to encourage this train of thought)

Candidate: "So........, I could ask a nurse what drugs she was taking?"

Interviewer: "Or...." (examiner looks hopeful)

Candidate: "Or......, I could look at the drug chart"

Interviewer: "Excellent. She normally takes low dose aspirin, an ACE inhibitor and insulin twice a day"

Candidate: "Oh (looks surprised), you didn't say she was diabetic!"

Interviewer: "You didn't ask (dead pan). Does that give you any more ideas as to possible causes for post-operative hypotension?"

Candidate: Looking somewhat flustered. "Hypoglycaemia?"

Interviewer: Shaking head "Her recent blood glucose is 5.6 mmol/L"

2.4
ii

Candidate: "???"

Interviewer: "..and if she complained of chest pain?"

Candidate: "Ohhh, heart attack. She could have had a heart attack. Or I suppose a PE"

Interviewer: "Yes, she has risk factors for both these complications. How might you explore these possibilities further?"

Candidate: "She needs ECG, Chest X-ray and V/Q scan"

Interviewer: "Well, possibly, if you thought these diagnoses were strong possibilities. Her blood results come back and show a haemoglobin of 5.1 g/dl. A nurse happened to request a clotting screen also. Her APTT is marginally raised and the electrolytes are normal. Mrs B now has a pulse of 124 per minute and her BP is 70/45. What would you do?"

Candidate: "I would request an urgent cross-match, and inform the medical registrar about the abnormal clotting result"

Interviewer: "Anyone else?"

Candidate: "I would call my registrar to help"

Interviewer: "The registrar is busy on labour ward. He tells you to call the on-call gynae consultant. What would you tell her?"

Candidate: "I would explain the situation, and await her advice"

Interviewer: "What do you think she will recommend?"

Candidate: "That the patient goes back to theatre"

Interviewer: "Yes. Who needs to be informed about this plan?"

Candidate: "The anaesthetist, and theatres"

Interviewer: "Anyone else?"

Candidate: Looks puzzled "Hmmmm…"

Interviewer: "The on-call haematologist?, a relative?, the woman herself?"

Candidate: "Yes. She needs consenting for laparotomy"

Interviewer: "Would you take consent for anything else?"

Candidate: "Hysterectomy….Er, no. She has had that already. I am not sure…"

Interviewer: "You should gain consent for blood transfusion, and the use of blood products. It is almost inevitable that this is going to be required.

Do you feel Mrs B has been adequately resuscitated? I don't think the anaesthetist will be very impressed when she arrives.

Candidate: "I am not sure that there is much else I could do……"

Interviewer: "I am concerned about the temperamental green cannula"

2.4
ii

Candidate: "Yes, she needs a grey or brown cannula. I forgot about that"

Interviewer: "And some supplemental oxygen".

On return to theatre, Mrs B is found to have over 1.5 litres of blood in her abdomen. The bleeding has come from one of the pedicles and it takes some time for the consultant to get it under control. Mrs B requires 8 units of blood, fresh frozen plasma and platelets. The anaesthetist decides that an overnight stay in ITU is safest. What complications might Mrs B at risk of now?"

Candidate: "A blood transfusion reaction? I suppose she might bleed again. Her infection risk is raised by the second laparotomy so I would treat her with antibiotics"

Interviewer: "Mrs B actually is a patient on one of the other gynae firms to yours. Does your involvement end there?"

Candidate: "I would visit her on the ward, and check that she is recovering OK"

Interviewer: "What do you learn most from near-miss cases like this?

Candidate: Looks confused "………Well, I suppose it stresses to me the importance of good surgical technique."

Interviewer: "Well………, OK. How then do you derive maximal learning from clinical situations like this one"

Candidate: "I try to remember them for the future"

Interviewer: "Thankyou. You can move onto the next station"

The Management of Post Operative Hypotension

iii - Key Points

Although the clinical scenario is based on a gynae ward, this problem is not specific to obstetrics and gynaecology. Major haemorrhage, whatever the cause, is likely to be managed in a similar way. This OSCE station therefore does not discriminate against those who have not done O & G as a foundation doctor, or in a previous SHO post.

Candidate A is organised in her approach, and in how she gives her answers. Candidate B is quite the opposite. There is no system, or planning. His answer suggests that he would also have a similarly sloppy and disorganised approach to the clinical problem when actually faced with it.

Candidate A remembers the basics; A, B, C of resuscitation and take a history and examine the patient. Candidate B has to be prompted to do these things, and to seek out relevant background information.

Candidate A answers the questions succinctly and offers up added relevant points of note. The answers need to be dragged out of candidate B who requires much prompting.

Candidate A clearly has a much better understanding of acute medicine. Candidate B's answer suggests a poor level of knowledge.

Candidate A is able to produce a differential diagnosis for post-operative hypotension, and explain how she would work through this differential. The clues point strongly to primary haemorrhage and she is not easily distracted from this. Candidate B loses sight of the actual working diagnosis and is all too ready to suggest investigations which would be inappropriate in this acute scenario, such as VQ scan

Candidate A's answer suggests good communication skills and a team-based approach, unlike that of Candidate B. She states clearly what she thinks the problem is, and what she expects of the professionals she is liaising with. Candidate B doesn't even know himself what he wants to happen.

Candidate A demonstrates a mature and reflective approach to learning from critical incidents. Candidate B clearly misses the opportunity for feedback and adult-learning, and demonstrates no evidence that he is aware of the risk management process.

The Management of Post Operative Hypotension

iv - Marking Scheme

Scores are given across four domains; knowledge, communication skills, organisational skills and professional development.

For each variable assessed, a score of zero, 1 or 2 can be given. A score of 2 suggests that the candidate spontaneously offered the answer, without prompting, and that the answer was factually correct. A score of 1 is used if prompting was required, and the detail was mostly correct. A score of zero should be given if the candidate failed to give the correct answer, even with prompting, if the detail was incorrect, or if the candidate failed to demonstrate the skill or attribute being assessed.

KNOWLEDGE

1. Basic resuscitation skills	0	1	2
2. Differential diagnosis for post-operative hypotension	0	1	2
3. Post-operative complications	0	1	2

COMMUNICATION SKILLS

4. Multidisciplinary working	0	1	2
5. Team-working	0	1	2
6. Interaction with the patient	0	1	2

2.4
iv

ORGANISATIONAL SKILLS

7. Systematic approach to
   assessment in an emergency   0   1   2

8. Overall co-ordination
   of the clinical situation   0   1   2

PROFESSIONAL DEVELOPMENT

9. Reflective practice   0   1   2

10. Recognising the role
    of risk management   0   1   2

Appendix
Contact details for all the NHS Trusts in England & Wales.

Authorities and Trusts	Hospital Name	Area	Post Code	Telephone	Website
Aintree University Hospitals NHS Foundation Trust	University Hospital Aintree	Merseyside	L9 7AL	0151 525 5980	www.aintreehospitals.nhs.uk
Aintree University Hospitals NHS Foundation Trust	Walton Hospital	Merseyside	L9 1AE	0151 525 3611	
Airedale NHS Trust	Airedale General Hospital	Keighley	BD20 6TD	01535 652 511	www.airedale-trust.nhs.uk
Alder Hey Children's NHS Foundation Trust	Alder Hey Hospital	Merseyside	L12 2AP	0151 228 4811	www.alderhey.com
Alder Hey Children's NHS Foundation Trust	Liverpool Women's Hospital	Merseyside	L8 7SS	0151 708 9988	www.lwh.org.uk
Ashford and St Peter's Hospitals NHS Trust	St Peters Hospital	Surrey	KT16 0PZ	01932 872 000	www.ashfordstpeters.nhs.uk
Ashford and St Peter's Hospitals NHS Trust	Ashford Hospital	Middlesex	TW15 3AA	01784 884 488	www.ashfordstpeters.nhs.uk
Barking, Havering and Redbridge University Hospitals NHS Trust	Queens Hospital	Essex	RM7 0AG	0845 130 4204	www.bhrhospitals.nhs.uk
Barking, Havering and Redbridge University Hospitals NHS Trust	King George Hospital	Essex	IG3 8YB	020 8983 8000	www.bhrhospitals.nhs.uk
Barnet and Chase Farm Hospitals NHS Trust	Barnet Hospital	Hertfordshire	EN5 3DJ	0845 111 4000	www.bcf.nhs.uk
Barnet and Chase Farm Hospitals NHS Trust	Chase Farm Hospital	Middlesex	EN2 8JL	0845 111 4000	www.bcf.nhs.uk
Barnet and Chase Farm Hospials NHS Trust	Edgware Hospital	Middlesex	HA8 0AD	020 8366 6600	www.barnetandchase.nhs.uk
Barnsley Hospital NHS Foundation Trust	Barnsley District General Hospital	South Yorkshire	S75 2EP	01226 730 000	www.barnsleyhospital.nhs.uk
Barts and The London NHS Trust	The Royal London Hospital	Greater London	E1 1BB	020 7377 7000	www.bartsandthelondon.nhs.uk
Barts and The London NHS Trust	St Bartholomew's Hospital	Greater London	EC1A 7BE	020 7377 7000	www.bartsandthelondon.nhs.uk
Barts and The London NHS Trust	The London Chest Hospital	Greater London	E2 9JX	020 7377 7000	www.bartsandthelondon.nhs.uk
Basildon and Thurrock University Hospitals NHS Foundation Trust	Basildon University Hospital	Essex	SS16 5NL	0845 155 3111	www.basildonandthurrock.nhs.uk
Basildon and Thurrock University Hospitals NHS Foundation Trust	Orsett Hospital	Essex	RM16 3EU	0845 155 3111	www.basildonandthurrock.nhs.uk
Basildon and Thurrock University Hospitals NHS Foundation Trust	The Essex Cardiothoracic Centre	Essex	SS16 5NL	0845 155 3111	www.basildonandthurrock.nhs.uk
Basingstoke and North Hampshire NHS Foundation Trust	Basingstoke and North Hampshire Hospital	Hampshire	RG24 9NA	01256 473 202	www.northhampshire.nhs.uk
Bedford Hospital NHS Trust	Bedford Hospital South Wing	Bedfordshire	MK42 9DJ	01234 355 122	www.bedfordhospital.nhs.uk
Bedford Hospital NHS Trust	Bedford Hospital North Wing	Bedfordshire	MK40 2NS	01234 355 122	www.bedfordhospital.nhs.uk
Birmingham Children's Hospital NHS Foundation Trust	Birmingham Children's Hospital	West Midlands	B4 6NH	0121 333 9999	
Birmingham Women's NHS Foundation Trust	Birmingham Womens Hospital	West Midlands	B15 2TG	0121 472 1377	
Blackpool, Fylde and Wyre Hospitals NHS Foundation Trust	Bispham Hospital Rehabilitation Unit	Lancashire	FY2 0FN	01253 655 901	www.bfwhospitals.nhs.uk
Blackpool, Fylde and Wyre Hospitals NHS Foundation Trust	Blackpool Victoria Hospital	Lancashire	FY3 8NR	01253 300 000	www.bfwhospitals.nhs.uk
Blackpool, Fylde and Wyre Hospitals NHS Foundation Trust	Clifton Hospital	Lancashire	FY8 1PB	01253 306 204	www.bfwhospitals.nhs.uk
Blackpool, Fylde and Wyre Hospitals NHS Foundation Trust	Fleetwood Hospital	Lancashire	FY7 6BE	01253 306 000	www.bfwhospitals.nhs.uk
Blackpool, Fylde and Wyre Hospitals NHS Foundation Trust	Wesham Hospital Rehabilitation Unit	Lancashire	PR4 3HA	01253 655 404	www.bfwhospitals.nhs.uk
Bradford Teaching Hospitals NHS Foundation Trust	Bradford Royal Infirmary	West Yorkshire	BD9 6RJ	01274 542 200	www.bradfordhospitals.nhs.uk
Bradford Teaching Hospitals NHS Foundation Trust	St Lukes Hospital	West Yorkshire	BD5 0NA	01274 734 744	www.bradfordhospitals.nhs.uk
Brighton and Sussex University Hospitals NHS Trust	Brighton General Hospital	East Sussex	BN2 3EW	01273 696 955	www.bsuh.nhs.uk
Brighton and Sussex University Hospitals NHS Trust	Lewes Victoria Hospital	East Sussex	BN7 1PF		
Brighton and Sussex University Hospitals NHS Trust	Princess Royal Hospital	West Sussex	RH16 4EX	01444 441 881	www.bsuh.nhs.uk
Brighton and Sussex University Hospitals NHS Trust	Royal Sussex County Hospital	East Sussex	BN2 5BE	01273 696 955	www.bsuh.nhs.uk
Brighton and Sussex University Hospitals NHS Trust	Sussex Eye Hospital	East Sussex	BN2 5BF	01273 606 126	www.bsuh.nhs.uk
Brighton and Sussex University Hospitals NHS Trust	The Royal Alexandra Children's Hospital	East Sussex	BN2 5BE	01273 696 955	www.bsuh.nhs.uk

125

Authorities and Trusts	Hospital Name	Area	Post Code	Telephone	Website
Buckinghamshire Hospitals NHS Trust	Amersham Hospital	Buckinghamshire	HP7 0JD	01494 526 161	www.buckinghamshirehospitals.nhs.uk/amersham-hospital.htm
Buckinghamshire Hospitals NHS Trust	Stoke Mandeville Hospital	Buckinghamshire	HP21 8AL	01296 315 000	www.buckinghamshirehospitals.nhs.uk/stoke-mandeville-hospital.htm
Buckinghamshire Hospitals NHS Trust	Wycombe Hospital	Buckinghamshire	HP11 2TT	01494 526 161	www.buckshospitals.nhs.uk
Burton Hospitals NHS Foundation Trust	Queen's Hospital	Staffordshire	DE13 0RB	01283 566 333	www.burtonhospitals.nhs.uk
Calderdale and Huddersfield NHS Foundation Trust	Calderdale Royal Hospital	West Yorkshire	HX3 0PW	01422 357 171	www.cht.nhs.uk
Calderdale and Huddersfield NHS Foundation Trust	Huddersfield Royal Infirmary	West Yorkshire	HD3 3EA	01484 342 000	www.cht.nhs.uk
Cambridge University Hospitals NHS Foundation Trust	Addenbrooke's Hospital	Cambridgeshire	CB2 0QQ	01223 245 151	www.addenbrookes.org.uk
Cambridge University Hospitals NHS Foundation Trust	Newmarket Hospital	Suffolk	CB8 7JG		
Cambridge University Hospitals NHS Foundation Trust	Royston Hospital	Hertfordshire	SG8 9EN	01763 242 134	
Cambridge University Hospitals NHS Foundation Trust	Saffron Walden Community Hospital	Essex	CB11 3HY		
Cambridge University Hospitals NHS Foundation Trust	Rosie Hospital	Cambridgeshire	CB2 2SW	01223 217 617	www.addenbrookes.org.uk/serv/clin/women/rosie1.html
Central Manchester University Hospitals NHS Foundation Trust	Manchester Royal Eye Hospital	Greater Manchester	M13 9WH	0161 276 1234	www.cmft.nhs.uk
Central Manchester University Hospitals NHS Foundation Trust	Manchester Royal Infirmary	Greater Manchester	M13 9WL	0161 276 1234	www.cmmc.nhs.uk
Central Manchester University Hospitals NHS Foundation Trust	Royal Manchester Children's Hospital	Greater Manchester	M13 9WL	0161 276 1234	www.cmft.nhs.uk
Central Manchester University Hospitals NHS Foundation Trust	St Mary's Hospital	Greater Manchester	M13 0JH	0161 276 1234	www.cmft.nhs.uk
Central Manchester University Hospitals NHS Foundation Trust	University Dental Hospital	Greater Manchester	M15 6FH	0161 275 6666	www.cmmc.nhs.uk
Chelsea and Westminster Hospital NHS Foundation Trust	Chelsea and Westminster Hospital	Greater London	SW10 9NH	020 8746 8000	www.chelwest.nhs.uk
Chesterfield Royal Hospital NHS Foundation Trust	Chesterfield Royal Hospital	Derbyshire	S44 5BL	01246 277 271	www.chesterfieldroyal.nhs.uk
City Hospitals Sunderland NHS Foundation Trust	Sunderland Royal Hospital	Tyne and Wear	SR4 7TP	0191 565 6256	www.sunderland.nhs.uk/chs
City Hospitals Sunderland NHS Foundation Trust	Sunderland Eye Infirmary	Tyne and Wear	SR2 9HP	0191 565 6256	www.sunderland.nhs.uk/chs
City Hospitals Sunderland NHS Foundation Trust	Ryhope General Hospital	Tyne and Wear	SR2 0LY	0191 565 6256	www.sunderland.nhs.uk/chs
Clatterbridge Centre For Oncology NHS Foundation Trust	Clatterbridge Centre For Oncology	Merseyside	CH63 4JY	0151 334 1155	www.ccotrust.nhs.uk
Colchester Hospital University NHS Foundation Trust	Colchester General Hospital	Essex	CO4 5JL	01206 747 474	www.colchesterhospital.nhs.uk
Colchester Hospital University NHS Foundation Trust	Essex County Hospital	Essex	CO3 3NB	01206 747 474	www.colchesterhospital.nhs.uk
Colchester Hospital University NHS Foundation Trust	Halstead Hospital	Essex	CO9 2DL	01787 291 022	www.colchesterhospital.nhs.uk
Colchester Hospital University NHS Foundation Trust	Clacton and District Hospital	Essex	CO15 1LH	01255 201 717	www.colchesterhospital.nhs.uk
Countess Of Chester Hospital NHS Foundation Trust	Countess Of Chester Hospital	Cheshire	CH2 1UL	01244 365 000	www.coch.nhs.uk
Countess Of Chester Hospital NHS Foundation Trust	Ellesmere Port Hospital	Merseyside	CH65 6SG	01244 365 000	www.wcheshirepct.nhs.uk
County Durham and Darlington NHS Foundation Trust	Darlington Memorial Hospital	County Durham	DL3 6HX	01325 380 100	www.cddft.nhs.uk
County Durham and Darlington NHS Foundation Trust	University Hospital Of North Durham	County Durham	DH1 5TW	0191 333 2333	www.cddft.nhs.uk
County Durham and Darlington NHS Foundation Trust	Bishop Auckland General Hospital	County Durham	DL14 6AD	01388 455 000	www.cddft.nhs.uk
County Durham and Darlington NHS Foundation Trust	Chester Le Street Hospital	County Durham	DH3 3AT	0191 333 2333	www.cddft.nhs.uk
County Durham and Darlington NHS Foundation Trust	Shotley Bridge Hospital	County Durham	DH8 0NB	0191 333 2333	www.cddft.nhs.uk
Dartford and Gravesham NHS Trust	Darent Valley Hospital	Kent	DA2 8DA	01322 428 100	www.dvh.nhs.uk
Dartford and Gravesham NHS Trust	Gravesham Community Hospital	Kent	DA11 0DG		
Derby Hospitals NHS Foundation Trust	Royal Derby Hospital	Derbyshire	DE22 3NE	01332 340 131	www.derbyhospitals.nhs.uk
Derby Hospitals NHS Foundation Trust	London Road Community Hospital	Derbyshire	DE1 2QY	01332 347 141	www.derbyhospitals.nhs.uk

Authorities and Trusts	Hospital Name	Area	Post Code	Telephone	Website
Doncaster and Bassetlaw Hospitals NHS Foundation Trust	Doncaster Royal Infirmary	South Yorkshire	DN2 5LT	01302 366 666	www.dbh.nhs.uk
Doncaster and Bassetlaw Hospitals NHS Foundation Trust	Bassetlaw Hospital	Nottinghamshire	S81 0BD	01909 500 990	www.dbh.nhs.uk
Doncaster and Bassetlaw Hospitals NHS Foundation Trust	Montagu Hospital	South Yorkshire	S64 0AZ	01709 585 171	www.dbh.nhs.uk
Doncaster and Bassetlaw Hospitals NHS Foundation Trust	Tickhill Road Hospital	South Yorkshire	DN4 8QN	01302 796 000	www.dbh.nhs.uk
Doncaster and Bassetlaw Hospitals NHS Foundation Trust	Retford Hospital	Nottinghamshire	DN22 7XF	01777 274 400	www.dbh.nhs.uk
Dorset County Hospital NHS Foundation Trust	Blandford Community Hospital	Dorset	DT11 7DD	01258 456 541	www.dorset-pct.nhs.uk
Dorset County Hospital NHS Foundation Trust	Bridport Community Hospital	Dorset	DT6 5DR	01308 422 371	www.dorset-pct.nhs.uk
Dorset County Hospital NHS Foundation Trust	Dorset County Hospital	Dorset	DT1 2JY	01305 251 150	www.dchft.nhs.uk
Dorset County Hospital NHS Foundation Trust	Portland Hospital	Dorset	DT5 1AX	01305 820 341	www.dorset-pct.nhs.uk
Dorset County Hospital NHS Foundation Trust	Yeatman Hospital	Dorset	DT9 3JU	01935 813 991	www.dorset-pct.nhs.uk
Dorset County Hospital NHS Foundation Trust	Weymouth Community Hospital	Dorset	DT4 7TB	01305 760 022	www.dorset-pct.nhs.uk
Ealing Hospital NHS Trust	Ealing Hospital	Middlesex	UB1 3HW	020 8967 5000	www.ealinghospital.nhs.uk
East and North Hertfordshire NHS Trust	Lister Hospital	Hertfordshire	SG1 4AB	01438 314 333	www.enherts-tr.nhs.uk
East and North Hertfordshire NHS Trust	Mount Vernon Cancer Centre	Middlesex	HA6 2RN	01923 826 111	www.enherts-tr.nhs.uk
East and North Hertfordshire NHS Trust	Queen Elizabeth I I Hospital	Hertfordshire	AL7 4HQ	01438 314 333	www.enherts-tr.nhs.uk
East and North Hertfordshire NHS Trust	Hertford County Hospital	Hertfordshire	SG14 1LP	01438 314 333	www.enherts-tr.nhs.uk
East Cheshire NHS Trust	Macclesfield District General Hospital	Cheshire	SK10 3BL	01625 421 000	www.eastcheshire.nhs.uk
East Cheshire NHS Trust	Congleton War Memorial Hospital	Cheshire	CW12 3AR	01260 294 800	www.eccheshire-tr.nwest.nhs.uk
East Cheshire NHS Trust	Knutsford and District Community Hospital	Cheshire	WA16 0BT	01565 757 220	www.eccheshire-tr.nwest.nhs.uk
East Kent Hospitals University NHS Foundation Trust	Queen Victoria Memorial Hospital (Herne Bay)	Kent	CT6 6EB	01227 594 700	
East Kent Hospitals University NHS Foundation Trust	Buckland Hospital	Kent	CT17 0HD	01304 201 624	http://www.ekhut.nhs.uk/home-page/patients-and-public/our-hospitals/buckland-hospital/
East Kent Hospitals University NHS Foundation Trust	Kent and Canterbury Hospital	Kent	CT1 3NG	01227 766 877	http://www.ekhut.nhs.uk/home-page/patients-and-public/our-hospitals/kent-and-canterbury-hospital/
East Kent Hospitals University NHS Foundation Trust	Faversham Cottage Hospital	Kent	ME13 8PS		
East Kent Hospitals University NHS Foundation Trust	Queen Elizabeth The Queen Mother Hospital	Kent	CT9 4AN	01843 225 544	http://www.ekhut.nhs.uk/home-page/patients-and-public/our-hospitals/queen-elizabeth-the-queen-mother-hospital/
East Kent Hospitals University NHS Foundation Trust	Maidstone District General Hospital	Kent	ME16 9QQ	01622 729 000	www.mtw.nhs.uk
East Kent Hospitals University NHS Foundation Trust	Medway Hospital	Kent	ME7 5NY	01634 830 000	www.kentandmedway.nhs.uk
East Kent Hospitals University NHS Foundation Trust	Royal Victoria Hospital (Folkestone)	Kent	CT19 5BN	01303 850 202	http://www.ekhut.nhs.uk/home-page/patients-and-public/our-hospitals/royal-victoria-hospital/
East Kent Hospitals University NHS Foundation Trust	Sittingbourne Memorial Hospital	Kent	ME10 4DT	01795 418 300	www.kentandmedway.nhs.uk
East Kent Hospitals University NHS Foundation Trust	Victoria Hospital (Deal)	Kent	CT14 9UA	01304 865 400	
East Lancashire Hospitals NHS Trust	Burnley General Hospital	Lancashire	BB10 2PQ	01282 425 071	www.elht.nhs.uk
East Lancashire Hospitals NHS Trust	Royal Blackburn Hospital	Lancashire	BB2 3HH	01254 263 555	www.elht.nhs.uk
East Lancashire Hospitals NHS Trust	Pendle Community Hospital	Lancashire	BB9 9SZ	01282 425 071	www.elht.nhs.uk
East Lancashire Hospitals NHS Trust	Rossendale Hospital	Lancashire	BB4 6NE	01706 215 151	www.elht.nhs.uk
East Sussex Hospitals NHS Trust	Conquest Hospital	East Sussex	TN37 7RD	01424 755 255	www.esht.nhs.uk/conquest
East Sussex Hospitals NHS Trust	Eastbourne District General Hospital	East Sussex	BN21 2UD	01323 417 400	www.esht.nhs.uk/eastbournedgh

Authorities and Trusts	Hospital Name	Area	Post Code	Telephone	Website
East Sussex Hospitals NHS Trust	Bexhill Hospital	East Sussex	TN40 2DZ	01424 755 255	www.esht.nhs.uk
East Sussex Hospitals NHS Trust	Crowborough Birthing Centre	East Sussex	TN6 1HB	01892 652 284	www.esht.nhs.uk
Epsom and St Helier University Hospitals NHS Trust	St Helier Hospital	Surrey	SM5 1AA	020 8296 2000	www.epsom-sthelier.nhs.uk
Epsom and St Helier University Hospitals NHS Trust	Epsom Hospital	Surrey	KT18 7EG	01372 735 735	www.epsom-sthelier.nhs.uk
Epsom and St Helier University Hospitals NHS Trust	Sutton Hospital	Surrey	SM2 5NF	020 8296 2000	www.epsom-sthelier.nhs.uk
Epsom and St Helier University Hospitals NHS Trust	Queen Mary's Hospital For Children	Surrey	SM5 1AA	020 8296 2000	www.epsom-sthelier.nhs.uk
Epsom and St Helier University Hospitals NHS Trust	South West London Elective Orthopaedic Centre	Surrey	KT18 7EG	01372 735 800	www.swleoc.nhs.uk
Frimley Park Hospital NHS Foundation Trust	Farnham Hospital Outpatients Department	Surrey	GU9 9QL	01483 782 000	www.farnhamhospital.nhs.uk
Frimley Park Hospital NHS Foundation Trust	Frimley Park Hospital	Surrey	GU16 7UJ	01276 604 604	www.frimleypark.nhs.uk
Gateshead Health NHS Foundation Trust	Queen Elizabeth Hospital	Tyne and Wear	NE9 6SX	0191 482 0000	www.gatesheadhealth.nhs.uk
Gateshead Health NHS Foundation Trust	Bensham Hospital	Tyne and Wear	NE8 4YL	0191 482 0000	www.gatesheadhealth.nhs.uk
Gateshead Health NHS Foundation Trust	Dunston Hill Hospital	Tyne and Wear	NE11 9QT	0191 482 0000	www.gatesheadhealth.nhs.uk
George Eliot Hospital NHS Trust	George Eliot Hospital - Acute Services	Warwickshire	CV10 7DJ	02476 351 351	www.geh.nhs.uk
Gloucestershire Hospitals NHS Foundation Trust	Cheltenham General Hospital	Gloucestershire	GL53 7AN	08454 222 222	www.gloshospitals.nhs.uk
Gloucestershire Hospitals NHS Foundation Trust	Delancey Hospital	Gloucestershire	GL53 9DT	08454 222 222	www.gloshospitals.nhs.uk
Gloucestershire Hospitals NHS Foundation Trust	Gloucestershire Royal Hospital	Gloucestershire	GL1 3NN	08454 222 222	www.gloshospitals.nhs.uk
Gloucestershire Hospitals NHS Foundation Trust	Healthy Living Centre	Gloucestershire	GL51 7SU		
Gloucestershire Hospitals NHS Foundation Trust	Lydney and District Hospital	Gloucestershire	GL15 5JF		
Gloucestershire Hospitals NHS Foundation Trust	Moore Cottage Hospital	Gloucestershire	GL54 2AZ		
Gloucestershire Hospitals NHS Foundation Trust	Moreton-In-Marsh Hospital	Gloucestershire	GL56 0BS	01608 650 456	
Gloucestershire Hospitals NHS Foundation Trust	Newent Doctors Practice	Gloucestershire	GL18 1BA		
Gloucestershire Hospitals NHS Foundation Trust	Stroud General Hospital	Gloucestershire	GL5 2HY	01453 562 200	
Gloucestershire Hospitals NHS Foundation Trust	Tewkesbury General Hospital	Gloucestershire	GL20 5QN		
Great Ormond Street Hospital For Children NHS Trust	Great Ormond Street Hospital Central London Site	Greater London	WC1N 3JH	020 7405 9200	www.gosh.nhs.uk
Great Western Hospitals NHS Foundation Trust	The Brunel NHS Treatment Centre	Wiltshire	SN3 6BB	01793 646 464	www.gwhswindon.org.uk/sw2abtc01.php
Great Western Hospitals NHS Foundation Trust	The Great Western Hospital	Wiltshire	SN3 6BB	01793 604 020	www.gwh.nhs.uk
Great Western Hospitals NHS Foundation Trust	Trowbridge Community Hospital	Wiltshire	BA14 8PH	01225 752 558	
Great Western Hospitals NHS Foundation Trust	Fairford Hospital	Gloucestershire	GL7 4BB	01285 712 212	
Great Western Hospitals NHS Foundation Trust	Savernake Hospital	Wiltshire	SN8 3HL	01672 517 200	
Great Western Hospitals NHS Foundation Trust	Chippenham Community Hospital	Wiltshire	SN15 2AJ		
Guy's and St Thomas' NHS Foundation Trust	Guy's Hospital	Greater London	SE1 9RT	020 7188 7188	www.guysandstthomas.nhs.uk
Guy's and St Thomas' NHS Foundation Trust	St Thomas' Hospital	Greater London	SE1 7EH	020 7188 7188	www.guysandstthomas.nhs.uk
Harrogate and District NHS Foundation Trust	Harrogate District Hospital	North Yorkshire	HG2 7SX	01423 885 959	www.hdft.nhs.uk
Harrogate and District NHS Foundation Trust	Lascelles Younger Disabled Unit	North Yorkshire	HG1 4PA	01423 881 977	www.hdft.nhs.uk
Harrogate and District NHS Foundation Trust	Ripon and District Community Hospital	North Yorkshire	HG4 2PR	01765 602 546	www.nypct.nhs.uk
Heart Of England NHS Foundation Trust	Good Hope Hospital	West Midlands	B75 7RR	0121 424 2000	www.heartofengland.nhs.uk

128

Authorities and Trusts	Hospital Name	Area	Post Code	Telephone	Website
Heart Of England NHS Foundation Trust	Heartlands Hospital	West Midlands	B9 5SS	0121 424 2000	www.heartofengland.nhs.uk
Heart Of England NHS Foundation Trust	Solihull Hospital	West Midlands	B91 2JL	0121 424 2000	www.heartofengland.nhs.uk
Heatherwood and Wexham Park Hospitals NHS Foundation Trust	Wexham Park Hospital	Berkshire	SL2 4HL	01753 633 000	www.heatherwoodandwexham.nhs.uk
Heatherwood and Wexham Park Hospitals NHS Foundation Trust	Heatherwood Hospital	Berkshire	SL5 8AA	01344 623 333	www.heatherwoodandwexham.nhs.uk
Heatherwood and Wexham Park Hospitals NHS Foundation Trust	King Edward Vii Hospital	Berkshire	SL4 3DP	01753 860 441	www.royalberkshire.nhs.uk
Heatherwood and Wexham Park Hospitals NHS Foundation Trust	St Mark's Hospital	Berkshire	SL6 6DU	01628 632 012	www.heatherwoodandwexham.nhs.uk
Heatherwood and Wexham Park Hospitals NHS Foundation Trust	Chalfont's and Gerrards Cross Hospital	Buckinghamshire	SL9 9DR		
Hereford Hospitals NHS Trust	Hereford County Hospital	Herefordshire	HR1 2ER	01432 355 444	www.herefordhospital.nhs.uk
Hinchingbrooke Health Care NHS Trus	Hinchingbrooke Hospital	Cambridgeshire	PE29 6NT	01480 416 416	www.hinchingbrooke.nhs.uk
Hinchingbrooke Health Care NHS Trus	The Huntingdon NHS Treatment Centre	Cambridgeshire	PE29 6NT	01480 416 416	www.huntingdon.nhs.uk
Homerton University Hospital NHS Foundation Trust	Homerton University Hospital	Greater London	E9 6SR	020 8510 5555	www.homerton.nhs.uk
Hull and East Yorkshire Hospitals NHS Trust	Castle Hill Hospital	East Yorkshire	HU16 5JQ	01482 875 875	www.hey.nhs.uk
Hull and East Yorkshire Hospitals NHS Trust	Hull Royal Infirmary	East Yorkshire	HU3 2JZ	01482 875 875	www.hey.nhs.uk
Hull and East Yorkshire Hospitals NHS Trust	Princess Royal Hospital	East Yorkshire	HU8 9HE	01482 701 151	www.hey.nhs.uk
Hull and East Yorkshire Hospitals NHS Trust	Beverley Westwood Hospital	East Yorkshire	HU17 8BU	01482 303 589	
Imperial College Healthcare NHS Trust	St Mary's Hospital (HQ)	Greater London	W2 1NY	020 7886 6666	www.imperial.nhs.uk/stmarys/index.htm
Imperial College Healthcare NHS Trust	Charing Cross Hospital	Greater London	W6 8RF	020 8846 1234	www.imperial.nhs.uk/charingcross/index.htm
Imperial College Healthcare NHS Trust	Hammersmith Hospital	Greater London	W12 0HS	020 8383 1000	www.imperial.nhs.uk/hammersmith/index.htm
Imperial College Healthcare NHS Trust	Queen Charlotte's Hospital	Greater London	W12 0HS	020 8383 1111	www.imperial.nhs.uk/qcch/index.htm
Imperial College Healthcare NHS Trust	Western Eye Hospital	Greater London	NW1 5QH	020 7886 6666	www.imperial.nhs.uk/westerneye/index.htm
Ipswich Hospital NHS Trust	The Ipswich Hospital NHS Trust	Suffolk	IP4 5PD	01473 712 233	www.ipswichhospital.nhs.uk
Isle Of Wight NHS PCT	St Mary's Hospital	Isle Of Wight	PO30 5TG	01983 524 081	www.iow.nhs.uk
James Paget University Hospitals NHS Foundation Trust	James Paget Hospital	Great Yarmouth	NR31 6LA	01493 452 452	www.jpaget.nhs.uk
James Paget University Hospitals NHS Foundation Trust	Lowestoft and North Suffolk Hospital	Suffolk	NR32 1PT	01502 587 311	www.jpaget.co.uk
James Paget University Hospitals NHS Foundation Trust	Northgate Hospital	Norfolk	NR30 1BU	01493 452 452	www.jpaget.co.uk
Kettering General Hospital NHS Foundation Trust	Kettering General Hospital	Northamptonshire	NN16 8UZ	01536 492 000	www.kgh.nhs.uk
Kettering General Hospital NHS Foundation Trust	Nuffield Diagnostic Centre	Northamptonshire	NN17 2UW		www.kgh.nhs.uk
King's College Hospital NHS Foundation Trust	King's College Hospital	Greater London	SE5 9RS	020 3299 9000	www.kch.nhs.uk
Kingston Hospital NHS Trust	Kingston Hospital	Surrey	KT2 7QB	020 8546 7711	www.kingstonhospital.nhs.uk
Lancashire Teaching Hospitals NHS Foundation Trust	Chorley and South Ribble Hospital	Lancashire	PR7 1PP	01257 261 222	www.lancsteachinghospitals.nhs.uk
Lancashire Teaching Hospitals NHS Foundation Trust	Royal Preston Hospital	Lancashire	PR2 9HT	01772 716 565	www.lancsteachinghospitals.nhs.uk
Leeds Teaching Hospitals NHS Trust	Chapel Allerton Hospital	West Yorkshire	LS7 4SA	0113 262 3404	www.leedsth.nhs.uk
Leeds Teaching Hospitals NHS Trust	Leeds Dental Hospital	West Yorkshire	LS2 9LU	0113 244 0111	www.leedsth.nhs.uk
Leeds Teaching Hospitals NHS Trust	Leeds General Infirmary	West Yorkshire	LS1 3EX	0113 243 2799	www.leedsth.nhs.uk
Leeds Teaching Hospitals NHS Trust	Seacroft Hospital	West Yorkshire	LS14 6UH	0113 264 8164	www.leedsth.nhs.uk
Leeds Teaching Hospitals NHS Trust	St James's University Hospital	West Yorkshire	LS9 7TF	0113 243 3144	www.leedsth.nhs.uk
Leeds Teaching Hospitals NHS Trust	Wharfedale Hospital	West Yorkshire	LS21 2LY	01943 465 522	www.leedsth.nhs.uk

Authorities and Trusts	Hospital Name	Area	Post Code	Telephone	Website
Liverpool Heart and Chest Hospital NHS Trust	Liverpool Heart and Chest Hospital	Merseyside	L14 3PE	0151 228 1616	www.lhch.nhs.uk
Liverpool Women's NHS Foundation Trust	Liverpool Womens Hospital	Merseyside	L8 7SS	0151 708 9988	www.lwh.nhs.uk
Luton and Dunstable Hospital NHS Foundation Trust	Luton and Dunstable Hospital	Bedfordshire	LU4 0DZ	0845 127 0127	www.ldh.nhs.uk
Maidstone and Tunbridge Wells NHS Trust	Buckland Hospital	Kent	CT17 0HD	01304 201 624	www.ekhut.nhs.uk/home-page/patients-and-public/our-hospitals/buckland-hospital/
Maidstone and Tunbridge Wells NHS Trust	Edenbridge War Memorial Hospital	Kent	TN8 5DA		
Maidstone and Tunbridge Wells NHS Trust	Faversham Cottage Hospital	Kent	ME13 8PS		
Maidstone and Tunbridge Wells NHS Trust	Homoeopathic Hospital	Kent	TN1 1JU	01892 542 977	
Maidstone and Tunbridge Wells NHS Trust	Kent and Sussex Hospital	Kent	TN4 8AT	01892 526 111	www.mtw.nhs.uk
Maidstone and Tunbridge Wells NHS Trust	Maidstone District General Hospital	Kent	ME16 9QQ	01622 729 000	www.mtw.nhs.uk
Maidstone and Tunbridge Wells NHS Trust	Medway Maritime Hospital	Kent	ME7 5NY	01634 830 000	www.medway.nhs.uk
Maidstone and Tunbridge Wells NHS Trust	Pembury Hospital	Kent	TN2 4QJ	01892 823 535	www.mtw.nhs.uk
Maidstone and Tunbridge Wells NHS Trust	Preston Hall Hospital	Kent	ME20 7NJ	01622 710 161	
Maidstone and Tunbridge Wells NHS Trust	Qeqm Hospital	Kent	CT9 4AN	01843 225 544	www.ekhut.nhs.uk/home-page/patients-and-public/our-hospitals/queen-elizabeth-the-queen-mother-hospital/
Mayday Healthcare NHS Trust	Mayday University Hospital	Surrey	CR7 7YE	020 8401 3000	www.maydayhospital.nhs.uk
Mayday Healthcare NHS Trust	Purley War Memorial Hospital	Surrey	CR8 2YL	020 8401 3000	www.maydayhospital.nhs.uk
Medway NHS Foundation Trust	Gravesham Community Hospital	Kent	DA11 0DG		
Medway NHS Foundation Trust	Maidstone Hospital	Kent	ME16 9QQ	01622 729 000	www.kentandmedway.nhs.uk
Medway NHS Foundation Trust	Medway Maritime Hospital	Kent	ME7 5NY	01634 830 000	www.medway.nhs.uk
Medway NHS Foundation Trust	Sittingbourne Hospital	Kent	ME10 4DT	01795 418 300	www.kentandmedway.nhs.uk
Medway NHS Foundation Trust	Spire Alexandra Hospital	Kent	ME5 9PG	01634 687 166	
Mid Cheshire Hospitals NHS Foundation Trust	Leighton Hospital	Cheshire	CW1 4QJ	01270 255 141	www.mcht.nhs.uk
Mid Cheshire Hospitals NHS Foundation Trust	Victoria Infirmary	Cheshire	CW8 1AW	01606 564 000	www.mcht.nhs.uk
Mid Essex Hospital Services NHS Trust	Broomfield Hospital	Essex	CM1 7ET	0844 822 0002	www.meht.nhs.uk
Mid Essex Hospital Services NHS Trust	Chelmsford and Essex Hospital	Essex	CM2 0QH		
Mid Essex Hospital Services NHS Trust	St John's Hospital	Essex	CM2 9BG	0844 822 0002	www.meht.nhs.uk
Mid Essex Hospital Services NHS Trust	St Michael's Hospital	Essex	CM7 2QU	0844 811 8110	www.meht.nhs.uk
Mid Essex Hospital Services NHS Trust	St Peter's Hospital	Essex	CM9 6EG	0844 822 0002	
Mid Essex Hospital Services NHS Trust	William Julien Courtauld Hospital	Essex	CM7 2LJ	0844 822 0002	
Mid Staffordshire NHS Foundation Trust	Cannock Chase Hospital	Staffordshire	WS11 5XY	01543 572 757	www.midstaffs.nhs.uk
Mid Staffordshire NHS Foundation Trust	Stafford Hospital	Staffordshire	ST16 3SA	01785 257 731	www.midstaffs.nhs.uk
Mid Yorkshire Hospitals NHS Trust	Clayton Hospital	West Yorkshire	WF1 3JS	0844 811 8110	www.midyorks.nhs.uk
Mid Yorkshire Hospitals NHS Trust	Dewsbury and District Hospital	West Yorkshire	WF13 4HS	01924 512 000	www.midyorks.nhs.uk
Mid Yorkshire Hospitals NHS Trust	Pinderfields General Hospital	West Yorkshire	WF1 4DG	0844 811 8110	www.midyorks.nhs.uk
Mid Yorkshire Hospitals NHS Trust	Pontefract General Infirmary	West Yorkshire	WF8 1PL	0844 811 8110	www.midyorks.nhs.uk
Milton Keynes Hospital NHS Foundation Trust	Milton Keynes Hospital	Buckinghamshire	MK6 5LD	01908 660 033	www.mkhospital.nhs.uk
Moorfields Eye Hospital NHS Foundation Trust	Moorfields Eye Hospital	Greater London	EC1V 2PD	020 7253 3411	www.moorfields.nhs.uk

Authorities and Trusts	Hospital Name	Area	Post Code	Telephone	Website
Moorfields Eye Hospital NHS Foundation Trust	Moorfields At Ealing Hospital	Middlesex	UB1 3HW	020 8967 5766	www.moorfields.nhs.uk
Moorfields Eye Hospital NHS Foundation Trust	Moorfields At Mile End Hospital	Greater London	E1 4DG	020 7377 7820	www.moorfields.nhs.uk
Moorfields Eye Hospital NHS Foundation Trust	Moorfields At Northwick Park Hospital	Middlesex	HA1 3UJ	020 8869 3160	www.moorfields.nhs.uk
Moorfields Eye Hospital NHS Foundation Trust	Moorfields At Potters Bar Hospital	Hertfordshire	EN6 2RY	01707 646 422	www.moorfields.nhs.uk
Moorfields Eye Hospital NHS Foundation Trust	Moorfields At St Ann's Hospital	London	N15 3TH	020 7566 2841	www.moorfields.nhs.uk
Moorfields Eye Hospital NHS Foundation Trust	Moorfields At St George's Hospital	London	SW17 0QT	020 8725 5877	www.moorfields.nhs.uk
Moorfields Eye Hospital NHS Foundation Trust	Moorfields At Watford General Hospital	Hertfordshire	WD18 0HB	020 7566 2970	www.moorfields.nhs.uk
Moorfields Eye Hospital NHS Foundation Trust	Moorfields At Upney Lane Centre	Essex	IG11 9LX	020 8594 7131	www.moorfields.nhs.uk
Newham University Hospital NHS Trust	Gateway Surgical Centre	Greater London	E13 8SL	020 7055 5550	www.newhamuniversityhospital.nhs.uk
Newham University Hospital NHS Trust	Newham General Hospital	Greater London	E13 8SL	020 7476 4000	www.newhamuniversityhospital.nhs.uk
Norfolk and Norwich University Hospitals NHS Foundation Trust	Cromer Hospital	Norfolk	NR27 0BQ	01263 513 571	www.nnuh.nhs.uk
Norfolk and Norwich University Hospitals NHS Foundation Trust	Norfolk and Norwich University Hospital	Norfolk	NR4 7UY	01603 286 286	www.nnuh.nhs.uk
North Bristol NHS Trust	Frenchay Hospital	Avon	BS16 1LE	0117 970 1212	www.nbt.nhs.uk
North Bristol NHS Trust	Southmead Hospital	Avon	BS10 5NB	0117 950 5050	www.nbt.nhs.uk
North Bristol NHS Trust	Riverside Unit	Avon	BS16 2EW	0117 965 6061	www.nbt.nhs.uk
North Bristol NHS Trust	Cossham Hospital	Avon	BS15 1LF	0117 967 1661	www.nbt.nhs.uk
North Bristol NHS Trust	Thornbury Hospital	Avon	BS35 1DN	01454 412 636	www.nbt.nhs.uk
North Cumbria University Hospitals NHS Trust	Brampton War Memorial Hospital	Cumbria	CA8 1TX		
North Cumbria University Hospitals NHS Trust	Cockermouth Community Hospital	Cumbria	CA13 9HT	01900 822 226	
North Cumbria University Hospitals NHS Trust	Cumberland Infirmary	Cumbria	CA2 7HY	01228 523 444	www.ncuh.nhs.uk
North Cumbria University Hospitals NHS Trust	Haltwhistle War Memorial Hospital	Northumberland	NE49 9AJ	01434 320 225	www.northumbria.nhs.uk
North Cumbria University Hospitals NHS Trust	Mary Hewetson Cottage Hospital	Cumbria	CA12 5PH	01768 767 000	
North Cumbria University Hospitals NHS Trust	Millom Hospital	Cumbria	LA18 4BY		
North Cumbria University Hospitals NHS Trust	Penrith Hospital	Cumbria	CA11 8HX	01768 245 300	
North Cumbria University Hospitals NHS Trust	Ruth Lancaster James Hospital	Cumbria	CA9 3QX	01434 381 218	
North Cumbria University Hospitals NHS Trust	West Cumberland Hospital	Cumbria	CA28 8JG	01946 693 181	www.ncumbria.nhs.uk
North Cumbria University Hospitals NHS Trust	Wigton Hospital	Cumbria	CA7 9DD		
North Middlesex University Hospital NHS Trust	North Middlesex Hospital	Greater London	N18 1QX	020 8887 2000	www.northmid.nhs.uk
North Tees and Hartlepool NHS Foundation Trust	University Hospital Of North Tees	Cleveland	TS19 8PE	01642 617 617	www.nth.nhs.uk
North Tees and Hartlepool NHS Foundation Trust	University Hospital Of Hartlepool	Cleveland	TS24 9AH	01429 266 654	www.nth.nhs.uk
North Tees and Hartlepool NHS Foundation Trust	Peterlee Community Hospital	County Durham	SR8 5UQ	0191 586 3474	www.nth.nhs.uk
North West London Hospitals NHS Trust	Central Middlesex Hospital	Greater London	NW10 7NS	020 8965 5733	www.nwlh.nhs.uk
North West London Hospitals NHS Trust	Northwick Park Hospital	Middlesex	HA1 3UJ	020 8864 3232	www.nwlh.nhs.uk
North West London Hospitals NHS Trust	St Mark's Hospital	Middlesex	HA1 3UJ	020 8235 4000	www.stmarkshospital.org.uk
Northampton General Hospital NHS Trust	Northampton General Hospital (Acute)	Northamptonshire	NN1 5BD	01604 634 700	www.northamptongeneral.nhs.uk
Northern Devon Healthcare NHS Trust	Bideford Hospital	Devon	EX39 3AG	01237 420 200	www.northdevonhealth.nhs.uk

131

Authorities and Trusts	Hospital Name	Area	Post Code	Telephone	Website
Northern Devon Healthcare NHS Trust	Holsworthy Hospital	Devon	EX22 6JQ	01409 253 424	www.northdevonhealth.nhs.uk
Northern Devon Healthcare NHS Trust	Ilfracombe Tyrrell Hospital	Devon	EX34 8JF	01271 863 448	www.northdevonhealth.nhs.uk
Northern Devon Healthcare NHS Trust	South Molton Hospital	Devon	EX36 4DP	01769 572 164	www.northdevonhealth.nhs.uk
Northern Devon Healthcare NHS Trust	Torrington Hospital	Devon	EX38 7BJ	01805 622 208	www.northdevonhealth.nhs.uk
Northern Devon Healthcare NHS Trust	North Devon District Hospital	Devon	EX31 4JB	01271 322 577	www.northdevonhealth.nhs.uk
Northern Lincolnshire and Goole Hospitals NHS Foundation Trust	Diana, Princess Of Wales Hospital	North East Lincolnshire	DN33 2BA	01472 874 111	www.nlg.nhs.uk
Northern Lincolnshire and Goole Hospitals NHS Foundation Trust	Scunthorpe General Hospital	North Lincolnshire	DN15 7BH	01724 282 282	www.nlg.nhs.uk
Northern Lincolnshire and Goole Hospitals NHS Foundation Trust	Goole and District Hospital	North Humberside	DN14 6RX	01405 720 720	www.nlg.nhs.uk
Northumbria Healthcare NHS Foundation Trust	One To One Centre	Tyne and Wear	NE29 0SF	0191 297 9810	
Northumbria Healthcare NHS Foundation Trust	Alnwick Infirmary	Northumberland	NE66 2NS	0844 811 8111	www.northumbria.nhs.uk
Northumbria Healthcare NHS Foundation Trust	Berwick Infirmary	Northumberland	TD15 1LT	0844 811 8111	www.northumbria.nhs.uk
Northumbria Healthcare NHS Foundation Trust	Blyth Community Hospital	Northumberland	NE24 1DX	0844 811 8111	www.northumbria.nhs.uk
Northumbria Healthcare NHS Foundation Trust	Haltwhistle War Memorial Hospital	Northumberland	NE49 9AJ	01434 320 225	www.northumbria.nhs.uk
Northumbria Healthcare NHS Foundation Trust	Rothbury Community Hospital	Northumberland	NE65 7RW	01669 620 555	www.northumbria.nhs.uk
Northumbria Healthcare NHS Foundation Trust	Morpeth Cottage Hospital	Northumberland	NE61 2BT	0844 811 8111	www.northumbria.nhs.uk
Northumbria Healthcare NHS Foundation Trust	Sir G B Hunter Memorial Hospital	Tyne and Wear	NE28 7PB	0191 220 5953	www.northumbria.nhs.uk
Northumbria Healthcare NHS Foundation Trust	Wansbeck Hospital	Northumberland	NE63 9JJ	0844 811 8111	www.northumbria.nhs.uk
Northumbria Healthcare NHS Foundation Trust	Hexham General Hospital	Northumberland	NE46 1QJ	0844 811 8111	www.northumbria.nhs.uk
Nottingham University Hospitals NHS Trust	Nottingham City Hospital	Nottinghamshire	NG5 1PB	0115 969 1169	www.nuh.nhs.uk
Nottingham University Hospitals NHS Trust	Queen's Medical Centre Campus	Nottinghamshire	NG7 2UH	0115 924 9924	www.nuh.nhs.uk
Nuffield Orthopaedic Centre NHS Trust	Nuffield Orthopaedic Centre	Oxfordshire	OX3 7LD	01865 741 155	www.noc.nhs.uk
Oxford Radcliffe Hospitals NHS Trust	Churchill Hospital	Oxfordshire	OX3 7LJ	01865 741 841	www.oxfordradcliffe.nhs.uk/aboutus/hospitals/churchill.aspx
Oxford Radcliffe Hospitals NHS Trust	Horton General Hospital	Oxfordshire	OX16 9AL	01295 275 500	www.oxfordradcliffe.nhs.uk/aboutus/hospitals/horton.aspx
Oxford Radcliffe Hospitals NHS Trust	John Radcliffe Hospital	Oxfordshire	OX3 9DU	01865 741 166	www.oxfordradcliffe.nhs.uk/aboutus/hospitals/jr.aspx
Oxford Radcliffe Hospitals NHS Trust	Chipping Norton Hospital	Oxfordshire	OX7 5AJ	01608 648 450	
Oxford Radcliffe Hospitals NHS Trust	Wantage Hospital	Oxfordshire	OX12 7AS	01235 205 801	
Papworth Hospital NHS Foundation Trust	Papworth Hospital	Cambridgeshire	CB23 3RE	01480 830 541	www.papworthhospital.nhs.uk
Pennine Acute Hospitals NHS Trust	Royal Oldham Hospital	Lancashire	OL1 2JH	0161 624 0420	www.pat.nhs.uk
Pennine Acute Hospitals NHS Trust	North Manchester General Hospital	Greater Manchester	M8 5RB	0161 795 4567	www.pat.nhs.uk
Pennine Acute Hospitals NHS Trust	Rochdale Infirmary	Lancashire	OL12 0NB	01706 377 777	www.pat.nhs.uk
Pennine Acute Hospitals NHS Trust	Fairfield General Hospital	Lancashire	BL9 7TD	0161 764 6081	www.pat.nhs.uk
Pennine Acute Hospitals NHS Trust	Birch Hill Hospital	Lancashire	OL12 9QB	01706 377 777	www.pat.nhs.uk
Peterborough and Stamford Hospitals NHS Foundation Trust	Peterborough District Hospital	Cambridgeshire	PE3 6DA	01733 874 000	www.peterboroughandstamford.nhs.uk
Peterborough and Stamford Hospitals NHS Foundation Trust	Peterborough Maternity Unit	Cambridgeshire	PE3 6BP	01733 874 000	www.peterboroughandstamford.nhs.uk
Peterborough and Stamford Hospitals NHS Foundation Trust	Edith Cavell Hospital	Cambridgeshire	PE3 9GZ	01733 874 000	www.peterboroughandstamford.nhs.uk
Peterborough and Stamford Hospitals NHS Foundation Trust	Stamford and Rutland Hospital	Lincolnshire	PE9 1UA	01780 764 151	www.peterboroughandstamford.nhs.uk

Authorities and Trusts	Hospital Name	Area	Post Code	Telephone	Website
Plymouth Hospitals NHS Trust	Totnes Community Hospital	Devon	TQ9 5GH		www.plymouthospitals.nhs.uk
Plymouth Hospitals NHS Trust	Derriford Hospital	Devon	PL6 8DH	0845 155 8155	www.plymouthospitals.nhs.uk
Plymouth Hospitals NHS Trust	Royal Eye Infirmary	Devon	PL4 6PL	0845 155 8094	www.plymouthospitals.nhs.uk
Plymouth Hospitals NHS Trust	Scott Hospital	Devon	PL2 2PQ	0845 155 8174	www.plymouthospitals.nhs.uk
Plymouth Hospitals NHS Trust	Mount Gould Hospital	Devon	PL4 7QD	0845 155 8100	
Poole Hospital NHS Foundation Trust	Poole General Hospital NHS Trust HQ	Dorset	BH15 2JB	01202 665 511	www.poole.nhs.uk
Portsmouth Hospitals NHS Trust	Gosport War Memorial Hospital	Hampshire	PO12 3PW	023 9252 3651	www.childbirthchoices.co.uk
Portsmouth Hospitals NHS Trust	Petersfield Community Hospital	Hampshire	GU32 3LB	01730 262 415	www.childbirthchoices.co.uk
Portsmouth Hospitals NHS Trust	Queen Alexandra Hospital	Hampshire	PO6 3LY	023 9228 6000	www.porthosp.nhs.uk
Portsmouth Hospitals NHS Trust	St Mary's Hospital	Hampshire	PO3 6AD	023 9228 6000	www.porthosp.nhs.uk
Queen Victoria Hospital NHS Foundation Trust	Queen Victoria Hospital	West Sussex	RH19 3DZ	01342 414 000	www.qvh.nhs.uk
Queen Victoria Hospital NHS Foundation Trust	William Harvey Hospital	Kent	TN24 0LZ		
Robert Jones and Agnes Hunt Orthopaedic and District Hospital NHS Trust	Robert Jones and Agnes Hunt Orthopaedic Hospital	Shropshire	SY10 7AG	01691 404 000	www.rjah.nhs.uk
Royal Berkshire NHS Foundation Trust	Royal Berkshire Hospital	Berkshire	RG1 5AN	0118 322 5111	www.royalberkshire.nhs.uk
Royal Berkshire NHS Foundation Trust	West Berkshire Community Hospital	Thatcham	RG18 3AS	01635 273 300	www.berkshirewest-pct.nhs.uk
Royal Berkshire NHS Foundation Trust	King Edward Vii Hospital	Berkshire	SL4 3DP	01753 860 441	www.royalberkshire.nhs.uk
Royal Berkshire NHS Foundation Trust	Windsor Dialysis Centre	Windsor	SL4 5EH		
Royal Bolton Hospital NHS Foundation Trust	Royal Bolton Hospital	Lancashire	BL4 0JR	01204 390 390	www.boltonhospitals.nhs.uk
Royal Brompton and Harefield NHS Foundation Trust	Royal Brompton Hospital	Greater London	SW3 6NP	020 7352 8121	www.rbht.nhs.uk
Royal Brompton and Harefield NHS Foundation Trust	Harefield Hospital	Middlesex	UB9 6JH	01895 823 737	www.rbht.nhs.uk
Royal Cornwall Hospitals NHS Trust	Royal Cornwall Hospital (Treliske)	Cornwall	TR1 3LJ	01872 250 000	www.rcht.nhs.uk/RoyalCornwallHospitalsTrust
Royal Cornwall Hospitals NHS Trust	St Michael's Hospital	Cornwall	TR27 4JA	01736 753 234	www.rcht.nhs.uk/RoyalCornwallHospitalsTrust
Royal Cornwall Hospitals NHS Trust	West Cornwall Hospital (Penzance)	Cornwall	TR18 2PF	01736 874 000	www.rcht.nhs.uk/RoyalCornwallHospitalsTrust
Royal Devon and Exeter NHS Foundation Trust	Exmouth Hospital	Devon	EX8 2JN	01395 279 684	www.devonpct.nhs.uk
Royal Devon and Exeter NHS Foundation Trust	Heavitree Hospital	Devon	EX1 2ED	01392 411 611	www.rdehospital.nhs.uk
Royal Devon and Exeter NHS Foundation Trust	North Devon District Hospital	Devon	EX31 4JB	01271 322 577	www.northdevonhealth.nhs.uk
Royal Devon and Exeter NHS Foundation Trust	Royal Devon and Exeter Hospital (Wonford)	Devon	EX2 5DW	01392 411 611	www.rdehospital.nhs.uk
Royal Devon and Exeter NHS Foundation Trust	Scott Hospital	Devon	PL2 2PQ	0845 155 8174	www.plymouthospitals.nhs.uk
Royal Devon and Exeter NHS Foundation Trust	Tiverton and District Hospital	Devon	EX16 6NT	01884 235 400	www.devonpct.nhs.uk
Royal Devon and Exeter NHS Foundation Trust	Victoria Hospital (Sidmouth)	Devon	EX10 8EW	01395 512 482	www.devonpct.nhs.uk
Royal Devon and Exeter NHS Foundation Trust	Axminster Hospital	Devon	EX13 5DU	01297 630 400	www.devonpct.nhs.uk
Royal Free Hampstead NHS Trust	Mount Vernon Hospital	Middlesex	HA6 2RN	01923 826 111	www.thh.nhs.uk
Royal Free Hampstead NHS Trust	St. Albans City Hospital	Hertfordshire	AL3 5PN	01727 866 122	www.westhertshospitals.nhs.uk
Royal Free Hampstead NHS Trust	Watford General Hospital	Hertfordshire	WD18 0HB	01923 244 366	www.westhertshospitals.nhs.uk
Royal Free Hampstead NHS Trust	Royal Free Hospital	Greater London	NW3 2QG	020 7794 0500	www.royalfree.nhs.uk
Royal Free Hampstead NHS Trust	Royal National Throat, Nose and Ear Hospital	Greater London	WC1X 8DA	020 7915 1300	www.royalfree.nhs.uk

133

Authorities and Trusts	Hospital Name	Area	Post Code	Telephone	Website
Royal Free Hampstead NHS Trust	Finchley Memorial Hospital	Greater London	N12 0JE	020 8349 7500	www.barnet.nhs.uk
Royal Free Hampstead NHS Trust	Edgware Community Hospital	Middlesex	HA8 0AD	020 8952 2381	www.nwlh.nhs.uk
Royal Liverpool and Broadgreen University Hospitals NHS Trust	Warrington Hospital	Cheshire	WA5 1QG	01925 635 911	www.warringtonandhaltonhospitals.nhs.uk
Royal Liverpool and Broadgreen University Hospitals NHS Trust	The Royal Liverpool University Hospital	Merseyside	L7 8XP	0151 706 2000	www.rlbuht.nhs.uk
Royal Liverpool and Broadgreen University Hospitals NHS Trust	Royal Liverpool University Dental Hospital	Merseyside	L3 5PS	0151 706 2000	www.rlbuht.nhs.uk
Royal Liverpool and Broadgreen University Hospitals NHS Trust	Broadgreen Hospital	Merseyside	L14 3LB	0151 282 6000	www.rlbuht.nhs.uk
Royal Liverpool and Broadgreen University Hospitals NHS Trust	Sir Alfred Jones Memorial Hospital (Acute)	Liverpool	L19 8JZ	0151 494 3198	www.rlbuht.nhs.uk
Royal National Hospital For Rheumatic Diseases NHS Foundation Trust	Royal National Hospital For Rheumatic Diseases	Avon	BA1 1RL	01225 465 941	www.rnhrd.nhs.uk
Royal National Hospital For Rheumatic Diseases NHS Foundation Trust	Warminster Hospital	Wiltshire	BA12 8QS	01985 212 076	
Royal National Hospital For Rheumatic Diseases NHS Foundation Trust	Paulton Memorial Hospital	Bristol	BS39 7SB	01761 412 315	
Royal National Hospital For Rheumatic Diseases NHS Foundation Trust	Chippenham Hospital	Wiltshire	SN15 2AJ	01249 447 100	
Royal National Hospital For Rheumatic Diseases NHS Foundation Trust	Devizes Hospital	Wiltshire	SN10 1EF	01380 723 511	
Royal National Hospital For Rheumatic Diseases NHS Foundation Trust	Frome Victoria Hospital	Somerset	BA11 1EY	01373 463 591	www.somerset.nhs.uk
Royal National Orthopaedic Hospital NHS Trust	The Royal National Orthopaedic Hospital	Middlesex	HA7 4LP	020 8954 2300	www.rnoh.nhs.uk
Royal National Orthopaedic Hospital NHS Trust	Royal National Orthopaedic Hospital	Greater London	W1W 5AQ	020 8954 2300	www.rnoh.nhs.uk
Royal Surrey County Hospital NHS Trust	Farnham Hospital	Surrey	GU9 9QL	01483 782 000	www.farnhamhospital.nhs.uk
Royal Surrey County Hospital NHS Trust	Haslemere Hospital	Surrey	GU27 2BJ	01483 782 000	
Royal Surrey County Hospital NHS Trust	Royal Surrey County Hospital	Surrey	GU2 7XX	01483 571 122	www.royalsurrey.nhs.uk
Royal United Hospital Bath NHS Trust	Bradford On Avon Community Hospital	Wiltshire	BA15 1TA		
Royal United Hospital Bath NHS Trust	Chippenham Hospital	Wiltshire	SN15 2AJ	01249 447 100	
Royal United Hospital Bath NHS Trust	Devizes Hospital	Wiltshire	SN10 1EF	01380 723 511	
Royal United Hospital Bath NHS Trust	Frome Victoria Hospital	Somerset	BA11 1EY	01373 463 591	www.somerset.nhs.uk
Royal United Hospital Bath NHS Trust	Melksham Hospital	Wiltshire	SN12 7NZ	01225 701 000	www.ruh.nhs.uk
Royal United Hospital Bath NHS Trust	Paulton Memorial Hospital	Avon	BS39 7SB	01761 412 315	
Royal United Hospital Bath NHS Trust	Royal United Hospital	Avon	BA1 3NG	01225 428 331	www.ruh.nhs.uk
Royal United Hospital Bath NHS Trust	Shepton Mallet Community Hospital	Somerset	BA4 4PG	01749 342 931	www.somerset.nhs.uk
Royal United Hospital Bath NHS Trust	Trowbridge Hospital	Wiltshire	BA14 8PH	01225 752 558	
Royal United Hospital Bath NHS Trust	Warminster Hospital	Wiltshire	BA12 8QS	01985 21 2076	
Salford Royal NHS Foundation Trust	Salford Royal	Greater Manchester	M6 8HD	0161 789 7373	www.srft.nhs.uk
Salisbury NHS Foundation Trust	Salisbury District Hospital	Wiltshire	SP2 8BJ	01722 336 262	www.salisbury.nhs.uk
Sandwell and West Birmingham Hospitals NHS Trust	City Hospital	West Midlands	B18 7QH	0121 554 3801	www.swbh.nhs.uk
Sandwell and West Birmingham Hospitals NHS Trust	Birmingham Midland Eye Centre (Bmec)	West Midlands	B18 7QH	0121 554 3801	www.swbh.nhs.uk
Sandwell and West Birmingham Hospitals NHS Trust	Sandwell General Hospital	West Midlands	B71 4HJ	0121 553 1831	www.swbh.nhs.uk
Sandwell and West Birmingham Hospitals NHS Trust	Rowley Regis Hospital	West Midlands	B65 8DA	0121 553 1831	www.swbh.nhs.uk

Authorities and Trusts	Hospital Name	Area	Post Code	Telephone	Website
Sandwell and West Birmingham Hospitals NHS Trust	Birmingham Treatment Centre	West Midlands	B18 7QH	0121 507 6180	www.swbh.nhs.uk
Scarborough and North East Yorkshire Health Care NHS Trust	Bridlington and District Hospital	North Humberside	YO16 4QP	01723 368 111	www.scarborough.nhs.uk
Scarborough and North East Yorkshire Health Care NHS Trust	Malton Community Hospital	North Yorkshire	YO17 7NG	01653 693 041	www.scarborough.nhs.uk
Scarborough and North East Yorkshire Health Care NHS Trust	Scarborough General Hospital	North Yorkshire	YO12 6QL	01723 368 111	www.scarborough.nhs.uk
Scarborough and North East Yorkshire Health Care NHS Trust	Whitby Community Hospital	North Yorkshire	YO21 1EE	01947 604 851	www.scarborough.nhs.uk
Sheffield Children's NHS Foundation Trust	Sheffield Children's Hospital	South Yorkshire	S10 2TH	0114 271 7000	www.sheffieldchildrens.nhs.uk
Sheffield Children's NHS Foundation Trust	Oakwood Young Peoples Centre	South Yorkshire	S5 7AU	0114 271 7000	www.sheffieldchildrens.nhs.uk
Sheffield Teaching Hospitals NHS Foundation Trust	Northern General Hospital	South Yorkshire	S5 7AU	0114 243 4343	www.sth.nhs.uk
Sheffield Teaching Hospitals NHS Foundation Trust	Royal Hallamshire Hospital	South Yorkshire	S10 2JF	0114 271 1900	www.sth.nhs.uk
Sheffield Teaching Hospitals NHS Foundation Trust	Weston Park Hospital	South Yorkshire	S10 2SJ	0114 226 5000	www.sth.nhs.uk
Sheffield Teaching Hospitals NHS Foundation Trust	Charles Clifford Dental Hospital	South Yorkshire	S10 2SZ	0114 271 7800	www.sth.nhs.uk
Sherwood Forest Hospitals NHS Foundation Trust	Ashfield Community Hospital	Nottinghamshire	NG17 7AE	01623 785 050	
Sherwood Forest Hospitals NHS Foundation Trust	King's Mill Hospital	Nottinghamshire	NG17 4JL	01623 622 515	
Sherwood Forest Hospitals NHS Foundation Trust	Mansfield Community Hospital	Nottinghamshire	NG18 5QJ	01623 785 050	
Sherwood Forest Hospitals NHS Foundation Trust	Newark Hospital	Nottinghamshire	NG24 4DE	01636 681 681	
Shrewsbury and Telford Hospital NHS Trust	Royal Shrewsbury Hospital	Shropshire	SY3 8XQ	01743 261 000	www.sfh-tr.nhs.uk
Shrewsbury and Telford Hospital NHS Trust	The Princess Royal Hospital	Telford	TF1 6TF	01952 641 222	www.sath.nhs.uk
Shrewsbury and Telford Hospital NHS Trust	Bridgnorth Hospital (Maternity)	Shropshire	WV16 4EU	01746 711 060	www.sath.nhs.uk
Shrewsbury and Telford Hospital NHS Trust	Ludlow Hospital (Maternity)	Shropshire	SY8 1QX	01584 872 201	www.sath.nhs.uk
South Devon Healthcare NHS Foundation Trust	Torbay Hospital	Devon	TQ2 7AA	01803 614 567	www.sdhct.nhs.uk
South Downs Health NHS Trust	Brighton General Hospital	East Sussex	BN2 3EW	01273 696 011	www.southdowns.nhs.uk
South London Healthcare NHS Trust	Queen Mary's Hospital Sidcup	Kent	DA14 6LT	020 8302 2678	www.slh.nhs.uk
South London Healthcare NHS Trust	Princess Royal University Hospital	Kent	BR6 8ND	01689 863 000	www.slh.nhs.uk
South London Healthcare NHS Trust	Queen Elizabeth Hospital Woolwich	Greater London	SE18 4QH	020 8836 6000	www.slh.nhs.uk
South London Healthcare NHS Trust	Orpington Hospital	Kent	BR6 9JU	01689 863 000	www.slh.nhs.uk
South London Healthcare NHS Trust	Erith and District Hospital	Kent	DA8 3EE	020 8308 3131	www.slh.nhs.uk
South London Healthcare NHS Trust	Beckenham Beacon	Kent	BR3 3QL	01689 863 000	www.slh.nhs.uk
South London Healthcare NHS Trust	Darent Valley Hospital	Kent	DA2 8DA		
South London Healthcare NHS Trust	Sevenoaks Hospital	Kent	TN13 3PG		
South Tees Hospitals NHS Foundation Trust	The James Cook University Hospital	Cleveland	TS4 3BW	01642 850 850	www.southtees.nhs.uk
South Tees Hospitals NHS Foundation Trust	Friarage Hospital	North Yorkshire	DL6 1JG	01609 779 911	
South Tyneside NHS Foundation Trust	South Tyneside District Hospital	Tyne and Wear	NE34 0PL	0191 404 1000	www.stft.nhs.uk
South Tyneside NHS Foundation Trust	Palmer Community Hospital	Tyne and Wear	NE32 3UX	0191 451 6000	www.stft.nhs.uk
South Tyneside NHS Foundation Trust	Primrose Hill Hospital	Tyne and Wear	NE32 5HA	0191 451 6375	www.sthct.nhs.uk
South Warwickshire General Hospitals NHS Trust	Stratford Hospital	Warwickshire	CV37 6NX	01789 205 831	www.warwickhospital.nhs.uk
South Warwickshire General Hospitals NHS Trust	Warwick Hospital	Warwickshire	CV34 5BW	01926 495 321	www.warwickhospital.nhs.uk

Authorities and Trusts	Hospital Name	Area	Post Code	Telephone	Website
Southampton University Hospitals NHS Trust	Southampton General Hospital	Hampshire	SO16 6YD	023 8077 7222	www.suht.nhs.uk
Southampton University Hospitals NHS Trust	Countess Mountbatten House	Southampton	SO30 3JB	023 8047 7414	www.suht.nhs.uk
Southampton University Hospitals NHS Trust	Princess Anne Hospital	Hampshire	SO16 5YA	023 8077 7222	www.suht.nhs.uk
Southampton University Hospitals NHS Trust	Ashurst Hospital	Hampshire	SO40 7AR	023 8074 7690	www.suht.nhs.uk
Southend University Hospital NHS Foundation Trust	Southend Hospital	Essex	SS0 0RY	01702 435 555	www.southend.nhs.uk
Southport and Ormskirk Hospital NHS Trust	Ormskirk and District General Hospital	Lancashire	L39 2AZ	01695 577 111	www.southportandormskirk.nhs.uk
Southport and Ormskirk Hospital NHS Trust	Southport and Formby District General Hospital	Merseyside	PR8 6PN	01704 547 471	www.southportandormskirk.nhs.uk
St George's Healthcare NHS Trust	St George's At St John's Therapy Centre	Greater London	SW11 1SW	020 8812 5385	www.stgeorges.nhs.uk
St George's Healthcare NHS Trust	St George's Hospital (Tooting)	Greater London	SW17 0QT	0208 672 1255	www.stgeorges.nhs.uk
St George's Healthcare NHS Trust	Bolingbroke Hospital	Greater London	SW11 6HN	020 8812 5370	www.stgeorges.nhs.uk
St Helens and Knowsley Hospitals NHS Trust	St Helens Hospital	Merseyside	WA9 3DA	01744 646 465	www.sthk.nhs.uk
St Helens and Knowsley Hospitals NHS Trust	Whiston Hospital	Merseyside	L35 5DR	0151 426 1600	www.sthk.nhs.uk
Stockport NHS Foundation Trust	Stepping Hill Hospital	Cheshire	SK2 7JE	0161 483 1010	www.stockport.nhs.uk
Stockport NHS Foundation Trust	Cherry Tree Hospital	Cheshire	SK2 7PZ	0161 483 1010	www.stockport.nhs.uk
Surrey and Sussex Healthcare NHS Trust	East Surrey Hospital	Surrey	RH1 5RH	01737 768 511	www.surreyandsussex.nhs.uk/sites/east_surrey
Surrey and Sussex Healthcare NHS Trust	Crawley Hospital	West Sussex	RH11 7DH	01293 600 300	www.surreyandsussex.nhs.uk/sites/crawley/
Surrey and Sussex Healthcare NHS Trust	Caterham Dene Hospital	Surrey	CR3 5RA	01883 837 500	
Surrey and Sussex Healthcare NHS Trust	Horsham Hospital	West Sussex	RH12 2DR	01403 227 000	
Tameside Hospital NHS Foundation Trust	Tameside General Hospital	Lancashire	OL6 9RW	0161 331 6000	www.tamesidehospital.nhs.uk
Taunton and Somerset NHS Foundation Trust	Musgrove Park Hospital	Somerset	TA1 5DA	01823 333 444	www.somerset.nhs.uk
The Christie NHS Foundation Trust	The Christie	Greater Manchester	M20 4BX	0161 446 3000	www.christie.nhs.uk
The Dudley Group Of Hospitals NHS Foundation Trust	Russells Hall Hospital	West Midlands	DY1 2HQ	01384 456 111	www.dgoh.nhs.uk
The Dudley Group Of Hospitals NHS Foundation Trust	Corbett Hospital	West Midlands	DY8 4JB	01384 456 111	www.dgoh.nhs.uk
The Dudley Group Of Hospitals NHS Foundation Trust	Guest Hospital	West Midlands	DY1 4SE	01384 456 111	www.dgoh.nhs.uk
The Hillingdon Hospital NHS Trust	Mount Vernon Hospital Site	Middlesex	HA6 2RN	01923 826 111	www.thh.nhs.uk
The Hillingdon Hospital NHS Trust	Hillingdon Hospital	Middlesex	UB8 3NN	01895 238 282	www.thh.nhs.uk
The Lewisham Hospital NHS Trust	University Hospital Lewisham	Greater London	SE13 6LH	020 8333 3000	
The Newcastle Upon Tyne Hospitals NHS Foundation Trust	Freeman Hospital	Newcastle Upon Tyne	NE7 7DN	0191 233 6161	www.newcastle-hospitals.nhs.uk
The Newcastle Upon Tyne Hospitals NHS Foundation Trust	Newcastle Dental Hospital	Tyne and Wear	NE2 4AZ	0191 233 6161	www.newcastle-hospitals.nhs.uk
The Newcastle Upon Tyne Hospitals NHS Foundation Trust	Newcastle General Hospital Acute Services	Tyne and Wear	NE4 6BE	0191 233 6161	www.newcastle-hospitals.nhs.uk
The Newcastle Upon Tyne Hospitals NHS Foundation Trust	Northern Centre For Cancer Care	Newcastle Upon Tyne	NE7 7DN	0191 233 6161	www.newcastle-hospitals.nhs.uk
The Newcastle Upon Tyne Hospitals NHS Foundation Trust	The Newcastle Fertility Centre	Tyne and Wear	NE1 3BZ	0191 219 4740	www.newcastle-hospitals.nhs.uk
The Newcastle Upon Tyne Hospitals NHS Foundation Trust	The Royal Victoria Infirmary	Tyne and Wear	NE1 4LP	0191 233 6161	www.newcastle-hospitals.nhs.uk
The Newcastle Upon Tyne Hospitals NHS Foundation Trust	Walkergate Hospital	Tyne and Wear	NE6 4QD	0191 233 6161	www.newcastle-hospitals.nhs.uk
The Princess Alexandra Hospital NHS Trust	Princess Alexandra Hospital	Essex	CM20 1QX	01279 444 455	www.pah.nhs.uk
The Princess Alexandra Hospital NHS Trust	St. Margaret's Hospital	Essex	CM16 6TN	01992 561 666	www.westessexpct.nhs.uk

Authorities and Trusts	Hospital Name	Area	Post Code	Telephone	Website
The Princess Alexandra Hospital NHS Trust	Herts and Essex Community Hospital	Hertfordshire	CM23 5JH	01279 444 455	www.qehkl.nhs.uk
The Queen Elizabeth Hospital King's Lynn NHS Trust	The Queen Elizabeth Hospital	Norfolk	PE30 4ET	01553 613 613	www.qehkl.nhs.uk
The Rotherham NHS Foundation Trust	Rotherham District General Hospital	South Yorkshire	S60 2UD	01709 820 000	www.rotherhamhospital.trent.nhs.uk
The Royal Bournemouth and Christchurch Hospitals NHS Foundation Trust	Royal Bournemouth General Hospital	Dorset	BH7 7DW	01202 303 626	www.rbch.nhs.uk
The Royal Bournemouth and Christchurch Hospitals NHS Foundation Trust	Christchurch Hospital	Dorset	BH23 2JX	01202 486 361	www.rbch.nhs.uk
The Royal Bournemouth and Christchurch Hospitals NHS Foundation Trust	Macmillan Unit	Christchurch	BH23 2JX	01202 705 470	www.rbch.nhs.uk/our_services/rehabilitation/macmillan_unit.shtml
The Royal Marsden NHS Foundation Trust	The Royal Marsden Hospital (London)	Greater London	SW3 6JJ	020 7352 8171	www.royalmarsden.nhs.uk
The Royal Marsden NHS Foundation Trust	The Royal Marsden Hospital (Surrey)	Surrey	SM2 5PT	020 8642 6011	www.royalmarsden.nhs.uk/mh
The Royal Orthopaedic Hospital NHS Foundation Trust	Royal Orthopaedic Hospital	Birmingham	B31 2AP	0121 685 4000	www.roh.nhs.uk
The Royal Wolverhampton Hospitals NHS Trust	New Cross Hospital	Wolverhampton	WV10 0QP	01902 307 999	www.royalwolverhamptonhospitals.nhs.uk
The Walton Centre NHS Foundation Trust	The Walton Centre For Neurology and Neurosurgery NHS Trust	Merseyside	L9 7LJ	0151 525 3611	www.thewaltoncentre.nhs.uk
The Whittington Hospital NHS Trust	The Whittington Hospital	Greater London	N19 5NF	020 7272 3070	www.whittington.nhs.uk
Trafford Healthcare NHS Trust	Trafford General Hospital	Greater Manchester	M41 5SL	0161 748 4022	www.trafford.nhs.uk
Trafford Healthcare NHS Trust	Altrincham General Hospital	Cheshire	WA14 1PE	0161 928 6111	www.trafford.nhs.uk
Trafford Healthcare NHS Trust	Stretford Memorial Hospital	Greater Manchester	M16 0DU	0161 881 5353	www.trafford.nhs.uk
University College London Hospitals NHS Foundation Trust	Hospital For Tropical Diseases	Greater London	WC1E 6JD	0845 155 5000	www.uclh.nhs.uk
University College London Hospitals NHS Foundation Trust	National Hospital For Neurology and Neurosciences	Greater London	WC1N 3BG	0845 155 5000	www.uclh.nhs.uk/Our+hospitals/National+Hospital+for+Neurology+and+Neurosurgery.htm
University College London Hospitals NHS Foundation Trust	Royal London Homeopathic Hospital	Greater London	WC1N 3HR	0845 155 5000	www.uclh.nhs.uk/Our+hospitals/Royal+London+Homoeopathic+Hospital.htm
University College London Hospitals NHS Foundation Trust	The Eastman Dental Hospital	Greater London	WC1X 8LD	020 7915 1000	
University College London Hospitals NHS Foundation Trust	The Heart Hospital	Greater London	W1G 8PH	020 7573 8888	
University College London Hospitals NHS Foundation Trust	University College Hospital	Greater London	NW1 2BU	0845 155 5000	www.uclh.nhs.uk
University Hospital Birmingham NHS Foundation Trust	Queen Elizabeth Hospital	West Midlands	B15 2TH	0121 472 1311	www.uhb.nhs.uk
University Hospital Birmingham NHS Foundation Trust	Selly Oak Hospital (Acute)	West Midlands	B29 6JD	0121 627 1627	www.uhb.nhs.uk
University Hospital Of North Staffordshire NHS Trust	University Hospital Of North Staffordshire	Staffordshire	ST4 7LN	01782 715 444	www.uhns.nhs.uk
University Hospital Of South Manchester NHS Foundation Trust	Wythenshawe Hospital	Greater Manchester	M23 9LT	0161 998 7070	www.uhsm.nhs.uk
University Hospital Of South Manchester NHS Foundation Trust	Withington Hospital	Greater Manchester	M20 2LR	0161 434 5555	www.uhsm.nhs.uk
University Hospitals Bristol NHS Foundation Trust	Bristol Eye Hospital	Avon	BS1 2LX	0117 923 0060	www.uhbristol.nhs.uk
University Hospitals Coventry and Warwickshire NHS Trust	University Hospital (Coventry)	West Midlands	CV2 2DX	024 7696 4000	www.uhcw.nhs.uk
University Hospitals Coventry and Warwickshire NHS Trust	Hospital Of St Cross	Warwickshire	CV22 5PX	01788 572 831	www.uhcw.nhs.uk
University Hospitals Of Leicester NHS Trust	Glenfield Hospital	Leicestershire	LE3 9QP	0300 303 1573	www.uhl-tr.nhs.uk
University Hospitals Of Leicester NHS Trust	Leicester General Hospital	Leicestershire	LE5 4PW	0300 303 1573	www.uhl-tr.nhs.uk
University Hospitals Of Leicester NHS Trust	Leicester Royal Infirmary	Leicestershire	LE1 5WW	0300 303 1573	www.uhl-tr.nhs.uk
University Hospitals Of Morecambe Bay NHS Trust	Westmorland General Hospital	Cumbria	LA9 7RG	01539 732 288	www.mbht.nhs.uk
University Hospitals Of Morecambe Bay NHS Trust	Queen Victoria Hospital	Lancashire	LA4 5NN	01524 405 700	www.mbht.nhs.uk

Authorities and Trusts	Hospital Name	Area	Post Code	Telephone	Website
University Hospitals Of Morecambe Bay NHS Trust	Royal Lancaster Infirmary	Lancashire	LA1 4RP	01524 65944	www.uhmb.nhs.uk
University Hospitals Of Morecambe Bay NHS Trust	Furness General Hospital	Cumbria	LA14 4LF	01229 870 870	www.mbht.nhs.uk
Walsall Hospitals NHS Trust	Manor Hospital	West Midlands	WS2 9PS	01922 721 172	
Warrington and Halton Hospitals NHS Foundation Trust	Warrington Hospital	Cheshire	WA5 1QG	01925 635 911	www.warringtonandhaltonhospitals.nhs.uk
Warrington and Halton Hospitals NHS Foundation Trust	Halton Hospital	Cheshire	WA7 2DA	01928 714 567	www.warringtonandhaltonhospitals.nhs.uk
Warrington and Halton Hospitals NHS Foundation Trust	Houghton Hall	Cheshire	WA2 0EA	01925 858 970	www.warringtonandhaltonhospitals.nhs.uk
West Hertfordshire Hospitals NHS Trust	Hemel Hempstead General Hospital	Hertfordshire	HP2 4AD	01442 213 141	www.westhertshospitals.nhs.uk
West Hertfordshire Hospitals NHS Trust	St Albans City Hospital	Hertfordshire	AL3 5PN	01727 866 122	www.westhertshospitals.nhs.uk
West Hertfordshire Hospitals NHS Trust	Watford General Hospital	Hertfordshire	WD18 0HB	01923 244 366	www.westhertshospitals.nhs.uk
West Middlesex University Hospital NHS Trust	West Middlesex University Hospital	Middlesex	TW7 6AF	020 8560 2121	www.west-middlesex-hospital.nhs.uk
West Suffolk Hospitals NHS Trust	West Suffolk Hospital	Suffolk	IP33 2QZ	01284 713 000	www.wsh.nhs.uk
Western Sussex Hospitals NHS Trust	St Richard's Hospital	West Sussex	PO19 6SE	01243 788 122	www.westernsussexhospitals.nhs.uk
Western Sussex Hospitals NHS Trust	Southlands Hospital	West Sussex	BN43 6TQ	01903 205 111	www.westernsussexhospitals.nhs.uk
Western Sussex Hospitals NHS Trust	Worthing Hospital	West Sussex	BN11 2DH	01903 205 111	www.westernsussexhospitals.nhs.uk
Weston Area Health NHS Trust	Children's Services South	North Somerset	BS23 3NT		
Weston Area Health NHS Trust	Weston General Hospital	Weston-Super-Mare	BS23 4TQ	01934 636 363	www.waht.nhs.uk
Whipps Cross University Hospital NHS Trust	Newham General Hospital	Greater London	E13 8SL	020 7476 4000	www.newhamuniversityhospital.nhs.uk
Whipps Cross University Hospital NHS Trust	Whipps Cross University Hospital	Greater London	E11 1NR	020 8539 5522	www.whippsx.nhs.uk
Winchester and Eastleigh Healthcare NHS Trust	Andover War Memorial Hospital	Hampshire	SP10 3LB	01264 358 811	www.wehct.nhs.uk
Winchester and Eastleigh Healthcare NHS Trust	Royal Hampshire County Hospital	Hampshire	SO22 5DG	01962 863 535	www.wehct.nhs.uk
Winchester and Eastleigh Healthcare NHS Trust	Winchester NHS Treatment Centre	Hampshire	SO22 5DG	01962 828 333	www.winchestertc.nhs.uk
Wirral University Teaching Hospital NHS Foundation Trust	Arrowe Park Hospital	Merseyside	CH49 5PE	0151 678 5111	www.whnt.nhs.uk
Wirral University Teaching Hospital NHS Foundation Trust	Clatterbridge Hospital	Merseyside	CH63 4JY	0151 334 4000	www.whnt.nhs.uk
Wirral University Teaching Hospital NHS Foundation Trust	St. Catherines Hospital	Merseyside	CH42 0LQ	0151 678 7272	www.whnt.nhs.uk
Worcestershire Acute Hospitals NHS Trust	Alexandra Hospital	Worcestershire	B98 7UB	01527 503 030	www.worcsacute.nhs.uk/alex
Worcestershire Acute Hospitals NHS Trust	Kidderminster Hospital	Worcestershire	DY11 6RJ	01562 823 424	www.worcsacute.nhs.uk/kidd
Worcestershire Acute Hospitals NHS Trust	Worcestershire Royal Hospital	Worcestershire	WR5 1DD	01905 763 333	www.worcsacute.nhs.uk/wrh
Wrightington, Wigan and Leigh NHS Foundation Trust	Royal Albert Edward Infirmary	Lancashire	WN1 2NN	01942 244 000	www.wiganleigh.nhs.uk/Internet/Home/Hospitals/raei.asp
Wrightington, Wigan and Leigh NHS Foundation Trust	Leigh Infirmary	Lancashire	WN7 1HS	01942 244 000	www.wiganleigh.nhs.uk/Internet/Home/Hospitals/leigh.asp
Wrightington, Wigan and Leigh NHS Foundation Trust	Thomas Linacre Outpatient Centre	Lancashire	WN1 1RU	01942 244 000	www.wiganleigh.nhs.uk/Internet/Home/Hospitals/tlc.asp
Wrightington, Wigan and Leigh NHS Foundation Trust	Wrightington Hospital	Lancashire	WN6 9EP	01942 244 000	www.wiganleigh.nhs.uk/Internet/Home/Hospitals/wrightington.asp
Yeovil District Hospital NHS Foundation Trust	Yeovil District Hospital	Somerset	BA21 4AT	01935 475 122	www.yeovilhospital.nhs.uk
York Hospitals NHS Foundation Trust	Selby and District War Memorial Hospital	North Yorkshire	YO8 9BX	01904 724 300	
York Hospitals NHS Foundation Trust	St Helens Rehabilitation Hospital	North Yorkshire	YO24 1HD	01904 724 626	
York Hospitals NHS Foundation Trust	White Cross Rehabilitation Hospital	North Yorkshire	YO31 8JR	01904 727 542	
York Hospitals NHS Foundation Trust	York Hospital	North Yorkshire	YO31 8HE	01904 631 313	www.yorkhospitals.nhs.uk